RED TO BLACK

Secrets of a Savvy CFO
To Run Your Business Successfully

Larry M. Cooper

10-10-10
Publishing

RedToBlack
Secrets of a Savvy CFO to Run Your Business Successfully
Larry M. Cooper

First 10-10-10 Publishing paperwork edition April 2019

Published by:
10-10-10 Publishing
Markham, Ontario

Table of Contents

Dedication

This book is dedicated to all the C-Suite executives and owner/managers who will be helped by this book. May this book provide you even a few good ideas/concepts to run your business more successfully.

To my parents, now departed, Max and Anne Cooper: I could never have been able to write such a book without your unending sacrifice to give my brother, Harvey, and me a better life. Dad, you always said that Harvey and I would get the education that you didn't, and so in writing this book, it has been put to good use. Mom, you were like a private teacher to us, helping us with our homework and, more importantly, teaching us a greater vocabulary, which has been put into great use here in this book.

To my departed girlfriend, Maxine Povering, because you thought the world of me, it gave me the confidence to write this book. You will always be cherished in my life.

To my family—brother, Harvey; sister-in-law, Deborah; nephew, Max; niece, Eve; and cousin, Michael—regardless of the frequency of our interactions, knowing that you always support me is more than enough to fulfill goals like writing this book.

To my departed sister, Rochelle, you taught me to appreciate and enjoy the smaller things in life.

Foreword

Are you an owner/manager or a C-Suite executive who needs to better understand the full financial aspects of your business? Are you a non-financial executive who doesn't know what you don't know about the financial affairs of business?

In *Red to Black*, author and CPA Larry M. Cooper tells you everything you need to know so that you can become more effective in your role, and grow your company profitably.

Larry has been a Chief Financial Officer (CFO) inside companies for almost his entire working career. He has worked in many different industries, in all sectors of the economy, operating in all of the different organizational structures (public, private, owner managed, multinational). Why is this important to you? Simply, he is a senior executive who has gained his experience in many different ways, in a variety of organizations, learning from a vast number of mentors throughout his career. He has many insights from this extensive array of knowledge, which he has assembled into an easy to read, practical compendium of topics to help you become more effective in your role.

This book is a must read. Very quickly, it will educate you on what you need to know about the financial affairs of your company, and how your finance department can best support you or your executive team. *Red to Black* will be a great reference source that you can use at any time.

To me the part that I best enjoyed was Larry's simple talk in plain, everyday language that is bereft of technical Accounting jargon. Larry shows that he understands Senior executives are not interested in a bunch of Accounting stuff that you don't see as having any relevance to you. He is a well seasoned Finance Executive who has been a key business partner with numerous C-Suite Executives and gets to the point of what they need to know and why.

Raymond Aaron
New York Times Bestselling Author

Chapter 1 – Starting a Company

What You Need

- Getting started
- Software
- Staffing
- Schedule for doing the books
- Checklist

Getting Started

This book is written on the premise that you have created some type of legal entity that will be the reporting vehicle for the business. This could be an incorporated company or a partnership, or some other legal structure. Please get proper legal and taxation advice for what is the best structure for your business. Don't skimp on this advice. (More on professional advisors, your team, later in the book.)

Regardless of the legal structure of your company, or any company, regardless of size, you need to keep a set of books. We have all heard this phrase, but what does it really mean? In simple terms, it is a set of records organized according to the standards that accountants learn, so that any knowledgeable financial person, upon seeing the financial records, knows what these records say.

There are a few fundamental aspects that are common to all sets of books:

- Reporting currency
- Account structure
- Accounting calendar

Reporting Currency: the currency in which the business conducts most of its transactions. As an example, a Canadian business operating in Canada, with mainly Canadian customers, will likely charge those customers in $CDN. The same business may or may not buy its products or services from suppliers in Canada or out of Canada, yet it would start with $CDN in its business and, as necessary, either pay in $CDN or buy other currencies (e.g., $US) using its $CDN. Therefore, we say its reporting currency is $CDN.

Account Structure: the list of accounts in your financial reporting system. There are typically both balance sheet and income statement accounts that, when taken together, form the basis for the financial statements. Every business will have a chart of accounts, where there are many accounts that are common, and some that are unique to the business or industry. This account structure will form the basis for preparing financial statements, so it is very important to do proper planning as to what you want reported monthly, to decide on these accounts at the beginning.

Accounting Calendar: the normal period of time that is reported on. In most cases, it is the calendar month. However, in the retail business, each week is seen as the same, so there are 52 reporting periods that are summarized into 13 financial reporting periods. This is done for comparable reporting at any time of the year.

The decision on these areas needs to be made prior to selecting your accounting software, to ensure that the software will fulfill your reporting requirements. In other words, if you wanted to do retail reporting, is the software able to handle 13 financial reporting periods without customization? If customization were required, this likely indicates that your choice of software is not the best match for your business, since you can probably find software that does not require customization.

It should be clear that the decision on setting up the books is not just an accounting exercise. You either need an experienced financial professional who knows and understands your business, or someone in senior management should be participating in the initial decision making to create the chart of accounts. I have seen numerous instances where the financial statements are produced, and someone in senior management wants to know about a certain expense in much greater detail than is being recorded in the chart of accounts. This oversight creates a large amount of work to go back to the base transactions and re-categorize them into this more detailed reporting. That is why it is wise to get senior management involved in the initial setup, to avoid redoing this type of work.

Software

It should be obvious that in today's times, any accounting department records will be using some type of accounting software. There is virtually no limit to the number of different software packages. Accordingly, it becomes extremely difficult to decide which accounting software will best serve the needs of your business. The most important recommendation I can give to you is that you recognize that the most important part of this decision must be done with thorough investigation and planning. This likely means consulting with colleagues, accounting advisors, and any other person you respect who may provide you with some useful information about the accounting software that they have experience with.

No accounting software is implemented effectively without a thorough plan. I am sure you have heard the phrase, *measure twice, saw once.* This is exactly the best piece of advice when choosing accounting software. Many businesses rush the implementation of accounting software, only to be disappointed by the performance once they're using it. Therefore, take heed to put together a plan with responsibilities and timelines that are realistic.

You will likely have many software experts present to you that their software solves all your business needs. You need some set of criteria to decide in an objective manner which software will best meet your needs. The best first step that I can recommend to you is to prepare a list of all the aspects of the accounting software that you want delivered for your business. When you are then considering different software packages, you would actually create a score sheet for each individual software, compared to your predetermined list. In this way, you will maintain your objectivity and be able to easily eliminate those software packages that clearly are insufficient for your business. This will also allow you to maintain your objectivity and not be swayed by effective sales people.

One area that I have experienced, which is probably the most effective to get you the best answer for your business, is talking to other users. The software company that you select will likely introduce you to some of their clients. This is a good start. Of course, there is an inherent bias. These companies, and individuals working in them, have been handpicked to talk with you, because they, in fact, are using that company's software, and have been happy with it. That doesn't mean that it is right for your business. Well before you start the process of investigating software packages, I encourage you to join some sort of user group, where you can meet like-minded people who are making the same evaluations, on an objective basis, with no bias. In this way, you will become educated well before you start meeting the software companies, and thus be in a better position ask the right questions.

Just to give you an indication of the wide variety of accounting software packages available, here is a brief list:

- QuickBooks
- Sage
- FreshBooks
- Xero
- Zoho
- Interact
- Wave
- SAP
- Dynamics Great Plains
- Blackbaud

My intent of listing this sample size of accounting software is to better enlighten you on the extensive amount of options. That is why a project to select accounting software is complicated. There are truly an extensive number of choices. It's for this reason that you must be well organized before you start the exercise; otherwise, you will likely be unduly influenced by good software salesmen. Not to put them down, but their job is to sell you their company software, and they will tell a very compelling story. Your job is to sift through this large quantity of information, and then boil it down to what will do the best for your company.

Staffing

In Chapter 9, I will provide an extensive discussion about the various types of positions in any finance department. At this early juncture in the book, I want to make you aware of the fundamental type of work that is required to be done by any finance department.

Every finance department, no matter what size, will have somebody in charge. For simplicity, I will call the top position in any finance department, Chief Financial Officer (CFO). The CFO is the most experienced and capable financial professional in your finance department. They are typically a certified professional accountant (CPA) for larger companies, but at a minimum, regardless of the size of your company, they have the requisite knowledge and experience of running the financial affairs of your company. Their key role is to provide financial leadership in your company, and supervise whatever staff are in the finance department.

The size of your company will be one of the key determinants of the number of staff in your finance department, and this will also determine how many people are doing what is referred to as the transaction processing. In simple terms, transaction processing means the actual recording of each transaction your business does into the accounting records.

There are typically two fundamental types of transactions: customers paying you, and you paying your suppliers, to whom you are a customer. Customers, who are paying you, are paying for the invoices that you have sent to them, for the product and/or service that was billed to them (accounts receivable). Payments that you make to your supplier are for goods and/or services that the supplier provided to you (accounts payable).

The staff who perform the work on accounts receivable and accounts payable are usually the most junior positions. Even in today's sophisticated state of computerization, the processing of accounts receivable and accounts payable still requires some form of clerical input and /or data entry.

Accordingly, that's why it is so important to select the most appropriate accounting software, so that you minimize the amount of transaction processing work. In past decades, accounting staff spent large parts of their time on accounting transactions. Given improvements in accounting software, it is an appropriate expectation that the transaction processing will be very simple and time effective for accounting staff in today's computerization environment, provided that you have selected the appropriate software for your business.

Schedule for Doing the Books

Every well-run finance department establishes a schedule for all its reporting. This should be the case for both internal and external reporting.

For external reporting, there are statutory requirements, but most well-run finance organizations should be reporting sooner than these minimum requirements. Aside from filing the reports that are required by the stock exchange with which the company is registered, most public companies will have some type of public media announcement of the results of the latest period. The most used method today is a webinar or public conference call, where the company management presents the latest results, comments/ explanations are made about the results, and there may or may not be time provided for questions from the audience. The audience consists of shareholders and any industry financial analysts who follow the company.

In order for a public company to achieve its public reporting schedule, its finance department will have developed a detailed schedule outlining all the steps and responsibilities needed to be completed before the public financial reporting is complete. This type of standard reporting can and should be done in private companies, even though any commitment to a schedule is not statutorily required. This is just good business practice.

Well-run finance departments will always challenge themselves to complete each month's preparation of the financial statements as quickly as possible. Accordingly, you will likely have heard your finance department talk about closing the books within 3 or 4 days of the month end. This objective is meant to focus your finance department to get done with the fundamentals of their duties, and allow for the maximum time to be spent on special projects and analysis each month. If you find your finance department still working on completing last month's financials, into the 3rd week of the month, you likely have at least one of these issues:

- Insufficient staffing in your finance department.
- Insufficient leadership in your finance function.
- Financial statements do not hold importance to senior management.
- Computer systems have not been modernized and, thus, finance staff does a lot of data stacking to get to the financial results.

Checklist

A checklist is a simple listing of all the key tasks that are done in a finance department. Each task should be thoroughly explained, either in the checklist itself or in some supporting document, so that any staff can read it and know what to do. Each task should have an assigned person responsible for said task, and for the timing of when the task should be completed.

Someone in the finance department should be assigned the responsibility of managing the checklist so that each step is being completed, logged when it's done, and followed up if it's not done on time. This serves two objectives:

1. Measures what you expect,
2. Provides factual information that may turn out to be helpful if tasks have not been completed according to the schedule.

These are the key areas that every finance department will likely be responsible for:

1. Ongoing monthly activities
2. Month-end activities
3. Monthly reporting
4. Monthly financial statements
5. Filing of any compliance reporting
6. Analysis
7. Ad hoc activities
8. Special projects

Now that you understand about actually keeping the books, you are ready to see what is actually done to put the actual company transactions into the books, in the next chapter.

Chapter Highlights

- Key issues to resolve to set up your accounting records.
- There are many choices when selecting accounting software. One of the best strategies I have seen is to join a user group and talk to many users of the software you are likely to implement, well before implementation.
- Basic staffing for any finance department. Understanding transaction processing.
- Every well-run finance department, whether in a public or private company, has a schedule of clear responsibilities and timing for all aspects of completing the monthly financial statements.

Chapter 2 – Keeping the Government Off Your Back

Compliance Activities

- Monthly or quarterly filings
- Sales tax returns
- Payroll preparation and reporting
- Internal controls

Monthly or Quarterly Filings

Every company has a different set of reporting requirements. The standard is typically monthly. Also, monthly usually means the normal calendar, so that there are 12 reporting periods in one year. In the retail business, reporting is typically done on a weekly basis and, therefore, a quarter is composed of 13 weeks, which means that there are two monthly periods of four weeks, and one monthly period of five weeks, for the total quarter.

Private companies usually have a choice of what their reporting period is. They could choose to report quarterly. This is possibly a bad business decision. Monthly reporting initiates a standard for good business practice. Good practice would be to report on a monthly basis to management, which provides them with timely financial feedback to better run their business. You should always use a monthly reporting period.

Public companies must report to their security body and their shareholders, quarterly. Public companies know that this is a minimum standard based on the regulations, but it is not how they operate the business. Effective management requires monthly reporting for management to take timely action on changes in business trends.

Sales Tax Returns

Most market-based economies have at least two levels of government, each of which may levy some type of consumption tax. In Canada, we have two major jurisdictions for sales tax. There is the federal level, and then each province (except for Alberta) has its own sales tax regime. The federal system is called the Goods and Services Tax (GST). It is levied on most goods and services at the rate of 5% of the value. Most of the provinces have harmonized with the federal government's Goods and Services Tax, such that the two jurisdictional taxes are combined and are referred to as the harmonized sales tax. In these cases where the taxes are harmonized, there is then only one reporting entity that a company must comply with for its sales tax reporting.

The intent of this book is not to be a major source of expertise on sales taxes, in Canada or any other jurisdiction, but rather to introduce you to the concepts; and you should find out further information that is specific to your company.

Each province has a different sales tax rate, which is applied to a different list of goods and services to determine the sales tax amount. In the harmonized sales tax regime, most of this has been made consistent to minimize the differences; however, there are still differences, and you must be knowledgeable for each province that your business operates in as to the specific rules of sales tax in that province.

Each province is very aggressive in protecting its sales tax base. Thus, there are clear rules as to which province a given sale is attached to for the purpose of sales tax reporting. It is essential that your company become very knowledgeable about this so that your reporting is done correctly and you are not subject to re-assessments.

The size of your company will determine the frequency of sales tax reporting. Most companies are required to file their sales tax reporting one month after the month for which they are reporting. Smaller companies may be able to report on a quarterly basis in the month after the end of a quarter. Again, each province will set its own rules as to frequency of reporting. Therefore, the specific rules need to be consulted.

The actual preparation of your monthly or quarterly sales tax return can only be completed effectively once you have closed that month's reporting in your financial system. It is for this reason that it is critical that the monthly close routine is efficient and done in a timely manner to ensure that you're able to report your monthly or quarterly sales tax reporting on time. The provincial and federal sales tax regimes are very efficient in monitoring your compliance to proper sales tax reporting. They have certainly implemented technology and computerization, such that missing returns or late returns are noticed very quickly after due dates, and you will start receiving reminder letters. The reminder letter by itself is not the concern; however, this can begin an escalation by a sales tax regime to start sending many reminders and phone calls. Even if you have done nothing wrong, the mere fact of being late becomes a distraction to your finance team. It veers you off course from your fundamental role as the custodian of the financial records for the company, and for reporting to management on results. And it's for this reason that sales tax returns should be done as quickly as possible after the financial records have been closed for the month or the quarter.

Payroll Preparation and Reporting

There are many different ways to handle payroll. Here are the main ones:

- Prepare it yourself (owner)
- Have your finance staff do it
- Hire a company that specializes in payroll processing
- Use online software

Regardless whether you have very few employees or many, it is my strong recommendation that you hire a payroll processing firm to handle the preparation of your payroll. The reason is simple. There are many different rules and regulations regarding deductions at source for employees, as well as for amounts that the employer is supposed to remit, which are becoming far too complicated for any one individual to know accurately. I have seen numerous errors on payroll by competent professionals who unfortunately were following rules that have become outdated and/or changed unbeknownst to them. This then causes potential reassessments by the Canada Revenue Agency (CRA), which can cause no end of grief and time to get corrected, as well as the potential black mark your company may have. Luckily, the cost to hire a professional payroll services provider is very small on a per employee basis, and it's well worth the investment. Even if you have your own finance staff, this still costs you money indirectly through the time they are spending, which would probably be better put elsewhere.

You should always have a new employee enrollment form that requires completion of all the basic information when they start: full employee name, status, full address, family contact information in the event of an emergency, car and license, social insurance number, full listing of all spouse/partner data and dependents, date of birth, and banking information if you are going to make direct deposits to their bank account. Aside from this information being needed in writing to ensure no misunderstandings, it is best in writing as evidence of no mistakes, and should be signed off by the department manager. This form thus becomes the basic input information for payroll to prepare each person's paycheck. When you have such a form, it makes it much easier to employ a payroll processing firm, and this is how you gain efficiencies that keep costs down, and most importantly, make for an efficient and accurate process.

Here is the list of likely organizations where there is a reporting relationship because of payroll:

- Employee
- CRA
- Provincial Treasurer for the province in which you reside
- Workman's compensation
- Employment insurance
- Canada pension
- Quebec pension (only in Quebec)

- Group benefits provider
- Your bank, if you pay employees directly to their bank

This list should clearly indicate to you the different organizations to which you have a responsibility to on behalf of your employee, which shows the relative complexity of payroll today.

Most firms have hired payroll processing companies for the very simple reason of the time that is consumed in the preparation of the payroll. Once the payroll has been prepared from whichever choice was made, that organization has the requirement to pay the employee for their earnings, less whatever withholdings are made (Canada pension, income taxes, group insurance benefits). In the interest of efficiency, it is wisest to have these amounts paid directly to the employee's bank account. There is also the requirement to pay the various withholdings to the particular organization to which they relate. As an example, the income tax amount withheld from your employee then needs to be remitted to CRA on behalf of your employee. This is another good example of why it is preferable to have a payroll processing company handle this on your behalf. They handle all the administration for this, rather than a member of your finance team, who is probably not a hundred percent well-versed in this, and would take a lot longer to do it than the payroll processing firm would.

I'm a big proponent of finding the most efficient and knowledgeable source to get tasks done, particularly repetitive tasks. Payroll is a perfect example of this, as the process itself does not change month to month, and you are hiring a processing firm, whose staff do this every day. Your staff would likely only be doing it once a month, and then, for every month, they would have to reorient themselves on some of the processes.

Internal Controls

Internal controls, in the accounting area of your company, are policies and procedures put in place to ensure the continued reliability of accounting systems and information. Accuracy and reliability are paramount in the accounting world. Without accurate accounting records, managers cannot make fully informed financial decisions, and financial reports can contain errors. Internal control procedures in accounting are each designed to minimize the possibility of fraud, and identify errors before they become problems.

Below are the typical areas of internal control, with commentary for each one.

Separation of Duties: This involves the splitting of duties that are incompatible, such as recording customer payments and taking the cheques to the bank. Provided you have enough staff, it is extremely wise to split duties so that one person does not do all the activities, and thus have the potential to make intentional mistakes or omissions, without anyone else noticing for long periods of time. When you hear of a fraud in a company, this is typically the fundamental reason that it was possible. One person had control over all the areas involving customer payments to the customers, and thus made intentional changes or omissions to cover up the actual fraud. Even in small companies with few finance staff, implement compensating controls. This means, for instance, if you only have one bookkeeper, who does everything, then you implement *compensating processes* to properly oversee this person. As an example, someone other than the bookkeeper would take the cheques to the bank, or someone else would review the bank statements to look for any suspicious entries.

It is noteworthy to mention that most frauds are committed by an internal employee, and are usually very clever and not easily detected. That is why the various controls noted in this section are so important. The controls do NOT provide a guarantee that there will be no fraud. There is no guarantee. Smart finance management implements the controls discussed here, which severely limits the likeliness of fraud. Please also note that even if you have an external audit by professional accountants, there is no assurance that they would find a fraud. In fact, in their engagement letter with the company, they will ask management to sign to the fact that management understands that the auditor, even if looking for fraud, gives no guarantee that they would find it. The engagement letter will state that it is management's responsibility to design processes and procedures to limit the likelihood of fraud.

Accounting System Access Controls: Each separate module in the accounting system (accounts receivable, accounts payable, general ledger) should have its own password and user access so that it is clear who has made what entries. Controlling access to different parts of an accounting system via passwords, lockouts, and electronic logs can keep unauthorized users out of the system, and also provide a way to audit the usage of the system to identify the source of errors/discrepancies.

Physical Count of Assets: The two largest assets, where a physical count of the assets is most relevant, is cash and inventory. Cash, because it is such a liquid asset, should be counted at the beginning and end of each shift, and reconciled to the proceeds from the sales reporting vs the actual cash in the cash register. It is a wise policy to hold employees accountable for cash shortages to ensure there is no incentive for cash shortage, and this should be tracked by employee to determine if there are any patterns. The largest physical asset in most businesses, except service business, is usually inventory. In this era of computerization, the physical count of inventory is probably done once per year, by counting the stock and matching it to the computer records. Any discrepancies (beyond trivial amounts) should be followed up, analysed, and reported on. Any large differences should have a cycle count (physical counts during the year, on a surprise basis, to compare a specific inventory stock keeping unit's (SKU) physical count to the computer record).

Depending on the industry, fixed assets should also be counted on a regular basis to ensure that all the fixed assets recorded on the books are in fact in possession of the company.

Standardized Financial Documents: It is best to use the same documents all the time for each type of transaction, so it is less likely to have mistakes.

Reconciliation of Sub Ledgers: The individual customer accounts are referred to as the accounts receivable sub ledger. The individual supplier records are referred to as the accounts payable sub ledger. Each month, there should be a reconciliation of both AR and AP sub ledgers to the general ledger. Any discrepancies should be followed up immediately, and explained and corrected.

Reconciliation of Bank Account: Comparing the bank statements to the banking information in the general ledger, should be done each month, and reconciled to the penny. You can have a 10-cent error, and say, "Who cares?" But what if two transactions are missing—$25,000.00 and $24,999.90? That's a 10-cent difference, yet what if one side is just delayed, but the other side has been manipulated. You will not find out, unless you reconcile to the penny. The bank reconciliation should be approved by a different person than the person preparing it.

General Ledger Account Analysis: All the GL accounts on the balance sheet should be reconciled at least quarterly. There can be items in a balance sheet account that require follow-up, but without the reconciliation being done, they can be forgotten. As an example, you prepay a convention for $10,000, and then, when the convention comes up, and the account is not reconciled, the payment is made again.

Budget Variances: When there are differences between the actual results vs budget, this is a key area in which finance departments can deliver value, by explaining the reasons/causals. This is where there is a deviation from management's original plans. Thus, there should be timely reporting on this, so corrective action can be taken.

Approval Authority: The finance department is the custodian of the company records but not the approver of individual transactions. The person/department manager should approve each transaction for which he/she has responsibility. Each person should have an approval limit, and transactions over that limit would require their boss to approve. This ensures that large transactions are approved by the person with the authority for the large transactions.

(Source of this info on internal controls: Some of it was obtained from an article by David Ingram, dated January 25, 2019.)

We have now covered the fundamentals about record keeping. In the next chapter, we start orientating this into important information for management, to run the business daily (cash flow).

Chapter Highlights

- Effective reporting requires monthly financial reporting.
- Most jurisdictions have a consumption tax, referred to as a sales tax. These sales taxes are unique to each jurisdiction. Thus, it is critical that the finance team learn the rules of their particular jurisdiction.
- There are many options available for payroll preparation and reporting. My advice is to hire a reputable payroll processing firm for this task.
- Internal controls, in the accounting area of your company, are policies and procedures put in place to ensure the continued reliability of accounting systems and information. Many different processes are outlined that improve internal controls, yet this does not preclude fraud. It is a management's responsibility to have the processes in place to minimize the possibility of fraud.

Chapter 3 – Cash is King

Cash Flow

- Recording customer payments
- Paying bills
- Components of cash flow – collections, disbursements
- Collections, managing customers
- Disbursements, expenses
- Daily, monthly cash flow forecasting
- Banking arrangements
- Financing

Recording Customer Payments

Recording of customer payments is generally referred to as collection of accounts receivable. There are two fundamental aspects in finance about receivables: collecting the money and then recording it in the customer's account.

This chapter is focused on the recording process and, therefore, will only speak to proper record-keeping for customers' accounts. Once a sale is made to your customer, it is typically invoiced the same day, or overnight. The goods/services are delivered, and the invoice for said product/service is generated. Any good financial software system should record this invoice into your customer's account to show the amount that has been invoiced, and that's the amount the customer owes you. The process of collecting this receivable from your customer is an art typically referred to as credit management, and we will speak to that in a later chapter.

When you receive the payment from your customer, it will usually come via a cheque payable to the company, a credit card payment, or some form of electronic banking amount sent to your bank account.

A fundamental principle of good customer record maintenance is that any amounts paid by your customer should be recorded immediately in their account with you. Although this may seem obvious, many firms handle this weekly or even monthly. This has the detrimental effect that if a customer calls your credit team, they would be unable to talk intelligently with a customer about whether the payment has been received. Therefore, if you wish to have a customer-centric organization, you will make the recording of customer payments to your company a top priority by your finance team.

When recording the payment by your customer again, in the interest of a customer-centric organization, you want to maintain the accounting of your records in the most simple and understood manner. This means that, hopefully, they paid the exact amount of the invoice and, therefore, you can clear the invoice with the payment from your records. However, if for any reason the amount paid is a different amount than the invoice, good record-keeping necessitates that you continue to show the invoice and the payment as separate items on the customer statement, until such time as the amount is resolved. In the interest of good customer relations, when such an occurrence happens, you want to follow up with that customer immediately to understand the reason for the different payment than your invoice. This is the smartest course of action that not only resolves all the issues quickly, but more importantly, limits customer upset and dissatisfaction. This is a good example of where your credit team helps you maintain good relations with your customers by acting promptly in a professional manner.

The common payment method by customers is still a bank cheque payable to your firm. This is the simplest because it is very clear on the cheque of who the customer is, Therefore, the finance staff are able to record it in the correct customer account.

The usage of cheques is becoming less common as more banking is done electronically. Accordingly, you need to have good processes in place to handle electronic banking that fulfills the principles outlined above of a timely recording of customer payments.

One of the newer methods of payment is referred to as an electronic funds transfer (EFT). This is a payment made by your customer, through their bank to your bank account directly. There is usually some method by which the customer will advise you which items are being paid. This is critical to ensure that you are able to record the customer payment accurately on their account. Unfortunately, although the actual money moves quickly and efficiently, the record-keeping part does seem to have its challenges. This is again another reason why your finance staff need to be recording these transactions on a daily basis and following up quickly. When there's any ambiguity about a receipt, it can be tracked down while everything is fresh in everyone's mind.

Some payments are made by credit card, and this can either be done online by the customer themselves, and/or by your staff taking the credit card information and then processing it through the various credit card processing firms. In these days of privacy, many companies do not wish to have that responsibility and, therefore, do not maintain the records of the customer's credit card number. The only place where a customer credit card number is maintained is with the credit card processing firm. Although this limits the privacy exposure of the firm, it does make you more reliant on the credit card processing firm, and less able to have the record you might need for proper recording of a credit card payment. It may be thought that because the customer paid immediately upon receipt, with a credit card, that recording the customer's credit card payment to their account is less time-sensitive. Although, conceptually, this is true, by waiting, there's the potential that again time causes any potential errors to be misunderstood and therefore hard to backtrack and correct. Thus, it is also critical that credit card payments are recorded on a customer's account in as timely a manner as possible—preferably daily.

Paying Bills

'Recording of payments is generally referred to as accounts payable. This is the act of you paying those people/companies who have provided goods/services to your company, and they are generally referred to as suppliers.

Most finance departments will have staff handling their vendor/supplier relationships to pay the invoice when due. In a similar manner as was described about the accounts receivable process, the accounts payable process is the same, except now your company is on the buying side of goods/services, and now pays to the vendor/supplier for what you received.

It is necessary to ensure you are only paying for goods/services that you wanted and are satisfied with. You need a process to verify that in fact that is what has taken place, before you make your payment. The best methodology is a purchase order system. In simple terms, it is the order that you have made. The size of your company will determine whether in fact you have a separate department, referred to as the purchasing department, handling this function. Also, the size of the company will determine whether you have a robust purchase order system and software. A system can be as simple as a phone call record, but that is very hard to verify after the fact, and so it is extremely advisable that any order of a product/service is done in writing, and this is the basis upon a purchase order system.

A purchase order system properly details all the various terms and conditions for the receipt of the goods/services. Once the good/service have been received, the purchase order is the standard to ensure that you are getting what you expect, and at the prices that you agreed to. The accounts payable (AP) department, in larger companies, does the matching of the supplier invoice with your purchase order to ensure that you are in fact receiving and paying for what you expected. In the event that there is any difference, AP shall go to the person in the ordering/purchase order department to indicate this difference, and it shall then be followed through with the supplier to be resolved. No payment should be made until the issue is resolved to your firm's satisfaction.

In the same way as in the accounts receivable system, where we keep track of each customer and the amount owing, we do the same for maintaining records of our invoices and payments to our suppliers. As already mentioned, we should not be paying an invoice until we are satisfied with the products/service and our price. This then causes the invoice in our accounts payable records to be cleared, as it is paid in full. Accounts payable should be recording supplier invoices as quickly as possible so that we can respond to any supplier/internal inquiries about the good/services, and be paying them according to the payment terms. It is also important that the accounts payable invoices are entered timely, so they get into the financial records to reflect accounting implications.

There was a major push in the 1980s and 1990s for companies to pay their bills electronically by something called EDI (electronic data interchange). Unfortunately, except in a few industries, this endeavor did not go very far, because companies on the accounts payable side said, "What's in it for me?" Given that there was no financial incentives or discounts to comply, few firms saw a benefit to effectively paying faster. The paying company would be paying faster because, in Canada, electronic payments through our banking system, for the most part, are in the receiving company's bank account the next day. This is much faster than the normal cheque mailed, which typically takes 3–5 days to arrive and be deposited in the bank of the receiving company. It was for this reason that EDI failed, because these payments would hit the bank account the next day, if not overnight, and most finance departments, on the payable side, were asking, "Why do I want to do that?"

Components of Cash Flow
– Collections, Disbursements

In its simplest form, cash flow is divided into two components:

* Collections – the money owed to you that you collect
* Disbursements – the money you owe others that you pay out

In finance, we have named these two components:

* Accounts Receivable – the amounts you charged for your product/service that you delivered, which you are now owed by your customers.
* Accounts Payable – the amounts you owe to your suppliers for the products/services you used/acquired. It should be noted that if you have employees, they are in essence *suppliers of labour* for your business, and should be considered as part of accounts payable for wages.

Managing cash flow, therefore, means collecting your accounts receivable in sufficient amounts so that you can pay your accounts payable, providing you are operationally profitable. If you are not operationally profitable, or are incurring capital expenditures, or have existing debt repayments, you will have needed a cash inflow from the shareholders, or arranged some type of new debt (long-term notes or some type of an operating bank line of credit—more on this in the financing section).

The fundamental principle of managing cash flow effectively is to collect more than you pay out, and not pay out in advance of your collections. (assuming you have financing available). This can be very challenging in struggling businesses, so I will share some concepts I have learned, to assist in this regard.

Collections, Managing Customers

In many companies, the credit department (This is the name usually given to the staff within the finance department whose responsibility it is to collect the accounts receivable.) is seen by the sales staff as wearing the black hat, because they chase their customers to pay their bills. Unfortunately, although technically correct, credit department staff are just ensuring that the company is paid for the services/products it delivered. No one within the company should have to apologize when calling/meeting customers to get them to pay for what has been delivered on the terms that were agreed upon prior to the delivery. However, some customers do not fulfill these terms, or they are in fact having financial difficulty. Credit staff that have the empathy with customers, while at the same time are able to secure the payment owed without creating bad feelings from the customers, are invaluable to a company. Good credit staff need to have the same customer orientation to service as sales staff to be effective. Even when the customer is not paying for what seems to be invalid reasons, and contrary to the terms agreed upon, they are still a customer, and thus need to be fully respected as the fulfillers of the wealth creation for the company. The most effective credit staff are those who not only have this customer orientation but work together with sales staff to secure the amounts owed. This means knowing your customer and being a facilitator for them of working with your company. There are many instances where a customer has issues with your company. It doesn't just have to be sales staff who resolve these types of issues. Credit staff can fulfill this function and thereby enhance their relationship with customers' staff. Credit staff who operate with a customer oriented mindset first, become problem solvers within your company, not just bill collectors.

Disbursements, Expenses

How strong are your controls on your disbursements? This is an area of your business that can be easy to monitor, and provides owners/ senior management quick oversight into how money is being spent in the business. I will not spend time here on purchasing systems, other than to say that to ensure money is spent wisely and for the best pricing available, you want a purchasing system that requires competitive quotes on any large purchases. The definition of large depends on the size of the business. Capital expenditures are one area that is usually large (over $5,000), and thus should have at least three quotes. This is especially appropriate because usually a capital expenditure is done infrequently. Thus, you need to be checking on prices in the market at the time of your purchase.

Ongoing purchases within the business are best handled by a quoting process, and then the best quote should be valid for at least one year, with this being repeated each year.

The process of accounts payable is to pay *authorized* purchases. These would be purchases as defined above, which have gone through the quoting process, or if they are too small, then the manager closest to the responsibility for the purchase should be signing the invoice, indicating their approval of the invoice. This approval means that this manager agrees that the goods/services were received as invoiced, and that the pricing is correct.

Accounts payable staff who then process invoices have the responsibility to match the authorized purchase documents and receiving documents as appropriate, and/or the manager's signed approval of the invoice before processing the invoice for payment. At this stage, the supplier invoice is now ready for payment. Accounts payable staff are typically at a junior level, and thus the CFO or the appropriate member of senior management determines the disbursement policy of when each supplier is to be paid, subject to funds being available. Any deviation from this policy needs that same senior management approval.

The actual signing of the cheque (if not automated) is a critical process to complete the disbursement cycle, add a layer of internal control, and provide senior management quick info as to how/where money is being spent. I can't count the number of times, when signing a cheque, I either found errors in the amount being paid, or gained insight into activities in the company that I was unaware of or only had a very cursory knowledge. The process of signing the cheque served as an info system to me, as

CFO, to make inquiries into the specific activity for which payment was being made, and thus be better informed for my job and/or provide valuable insights/suggestions.

In managing cash flow, many business people take the view to hold off paying bills until the credit department of the supplier calls enough times that you can't hold off any longer. This is a very win/lose mindset of running business. You have made an agreement with your supplier on terms, and should observe them, particularly if you have the financial ability to pay. This not only builds a win/win relationship, but if you are in the circumstance that you can't pay, you now have the credibility to talk directly and honestly with that credit department person to request some extended payment arrangements. This goes to the old axiom: "Build relationships early so they are there when you need them." This concept of talking to credit staff in an honest manner also reminds me of the favorite habit in accounts payable, which is to say, "The cheque is in the mail." This is again a very poor policy for you, as it destroys your company's creditability. Any good credit staff takes notes or tapes conversations, and thus they have it on file if you said the cheque was in the mail. When this doesn't occur, it becomes another mark against your credibility. Don't risk ruining your reputation for the sake of delaying a payment for a few days. However, always fulfill your promises; otherwise, don't make the promise. There is nothing that builds more credibility with credit staff than fulfilling your promises. Next time, they will believe you or be more flexible, if you request it with a promise of a delayed payment.

Daily, Monthly Cash Flow Forecasting

One of the best lessons I've ever learned on cash flow was to manage it daily. This may seem extreme, but I can tell you from experience that it was effective. This was actually a company that did not have any cash flow problems, but through meticulous planning and reporting philosophy, generated tremendous excess amounts of cash. You may ask, "How does the monthly reporting of cash generate more?" It starts with having a monthly cash forecast that is split into a daily cash forecast, for both receipts and collections. The chart is shown below.

Day of Month	Daily Collections	Daily Disbursements	MTD Collections	MTD Disbursements	Net Cash Position	Net Cash PLAN
1						
2						
.....						
Last day						
Total						

While simple in concept, it is powerful in its application. As already discussed, cash flow is the combination of receipts from customers, and disbursements to your suppliers. The wise management recognizes that its objective is to manage the net number, meaning the amount of collections less disbursements. Therefore, if for whatever reason you are not on target for your collections, it means you spend less. This simple reporting structure created a daily urgency for both the sales force and the credit team to collect money to provide the funds necessary for the planned disbursements. Therefore, this became a team exercise and not just a finance activity.

As a *fail-safe*, if collections were not being achieved, disbursements were held back until such time as collections caught up. This is just in keeping with proven management: "Don't spend what you don't have." You may be asking, "Didn't you say to pay your bills on time?" Yes. However, I also said that it is most important be honest with your suppliers' credit departments. For example, if in your own company your collections are not coming in on time, you would tell your suppliers' credit departments that you were a couple days delayed, until your collections come in. You are sure that this is just a timing issue and is in no way, shape, or form any indication of an actual financial problem.

Banking Arrangements

The phrase quoted, *"Keep your banker happy when times are good, because you will need them when times are bad,"* is the best advice I've ever seen about managing the banking relationship. Regardless of which bank you do business with, the reality is that the banking profession is very consistent across the board. Bankers fundamentally do not like risk for their bank. Therefore, it is in their job responsibilities to require you, as the Lendee, to provide more than adequate assets in the event you cannot pay your debt. In addition to this, there's the constant reinforcement to your banker, once the arrangements are put in place, to continue providing them assurance that not only are the assets much larger than the debt, but that in fact the ongoing operation is generating cash flow to pay back the debt in the agreed-upon manner.

Leaving aside the obvious performance requirement that you have a profitable business that is generating cash flow to pay your bank debt, what else is required? My best piece of advice is to practice a very open, transparent sharing with your banker about your business. This means at any time when there's anything of an unusual nature, don't wait for the banker to call you about it; initiate sharing the information with them, in both oral, and if necessary, written form. In addition, it is an extremely wise practice to conduct an annual review with your banker, updating about the past performance. Nothing endears you more to your banker than to tell them what you're going to do in your business, and then, a year later, not only achieve that but do better. The old adage quote, *"Under-promise, over-deliver,"* is especially true for your relationship with your banker.

Even during times when you are not in a borrowing position with your banker, the practice of updating them about your business, providing an annual review and constant information about your activities, is good business. In this way, when and if there's a need that you will require financing, they are totally in sync with where you are at in your business, and in fact are expecting it and are more likely coming to you, offering to loan you money. In summary, the best way to manage your banker is by good performance that has been consistently communicated.

Financing

This is not a book on financing, so I will not be going into the intricate details about each of these perspective finance vehicles. What is most important is choosing the financing format that most fits your business needs. This will be a combination of the amount of money needed, the risk that the lender is taking, the status of the business, and whether it is successful or struggling.

Finding the right financing for your business is like so many other aspects of running a business. Find the right expertise for the given circumstance. There are many independent consultants that can work with you and direct you to the right source, and I highly encourage you to do that if you do not already have the right internal expertise from your finance department. Many a business owner is hesitant to pay a consulting fee and/or a success fee to such consultants, and this is typical of the adage, *"Penny wise, pound foolish."* The amount that you will pay a consultant for his expertise/network to get the right financing for your business is a small amount compared to the amount of the financing required.

One key preparation note on financing: Don't wait until it is critical that you need the financing. Do your homework so that if there are periods where the business has a tight cash flow (for example, a seasonal business), you work well in advance of when you need the financing, and get it put in place. I had a situation in a business that had no revenue coming in over the summer months, yet the staff were working on the activities for the fall, and thus there was a significant cash outflow that needed to be funded. It was also a service business, so there were no assets that could be used as collateral. I started to seek the funding many months before it was required, so that the financing vehicle was in place well before the cash flow deficiency started.

In the next chapter, we introduce the centrepiece of what accountants are known for: preparation of financial statements, their format, and the typical usage.

Chapter Highlights

- An outline of all the nuances that come into play to record transactions on a customer account. Tips to make this simple and timely for the customer.
- Key features of your accounts payable system to make sure you are only paying for the purchases that your company has agreed to.
- Understanding the components of cash flow.
- Tips on collecting from customers and maintaining good relations.
- Paying bills is far more involved than just writing a cheque.
- Tips on managing vendor relationships.
- Managing cash flow is the combination of managing collections and paying bills, and how to manage this interrelationship.
- Financing is a topic that is a book in itself, so the discussion here highlights the complexities to understand, and recommends that you hire the experts in this highly sophisticated area of finance.

Chapter 4 – What's the Score

Financial Statements

- Timing of monthly financial statements, monthly close
- Flash sales
- Content of monthly financial statements
- Analysis
- Involvement of non-financial management
- Public reporting
- Reporting/presentation of financial statement in a private company

Timing of Monthly Financial Statements, Monthly Close

Every well-run finance department establishes a schedule for all its reporting. This should be the case for both internal and external reporting. Internal reporting is any reporting done within the company to the insiders, whereas external reporting is the reporting done to anyone not within the company. This includes securities commissions, shareholders, bankers, debt holders, and any person or entity to which the company provides financial information.

The first step in the preparation of financial statements is actually completing the financial reporting. In order to do this, all of the financial transactions for a given month need to be recorded in the financial records of the company. All good finance departments will establish a standard schedule of the various tasks and transactions to be done, and by who and by when. This is typically referred to as the monthly close schedule. For public companies, the close schedule is usually very compressed in the amount of time to get the financial statements done. Private companies, on the other hand, usually do not have the same discipline that is enforced, because of the public reporting. Therefore, their close schedule usually takes longer. In this regard, private companies can learn a lot from public companies by being much more disciplined in their financial close process, and getting the financial statements done.

The following is an example of a typical financial close schedule and the inherent parts:

Timing	Description
Last day of month	All product to be sold in the month has been packaged and shipped out. All invoicing for products or services is complete.
Month after the reporting month	
Day 1	All customer payments have been recorded in the customer's account. A flash sales report has been issued.
Day 2	All supplier invoices are recorded. Final sales reports have been issued.
Day 3	All bank reconciliations are complete.
Day 4	Draft 1 of the trial balance is produced. General ledger accounts are analysed as necessary. Journal entries are prepared and posted to the GL as necessary. All GL account reconciliations are completed.
Day 5	Draft 1 of the financial statements is produced in the morning. Financial commentary is prepared and reviewed by senior finance staff. As a result of the analysis and commentary, any adjustments/ corrections are made to financial statements. The final financial statement is produced by the end of the day.

Well-run finance departments will always challenge themselves to complete each month's preparation of the financial statements as quickly as possible. Accordingly, you will likely have heard your finance department talk about closing the books within 3 or 4 days of the month end. This objective is meant to focus your finance department to get done with the fundamentals of their duties, and allow for the maximum time to be spent on special projects and analysis each month. If you find your finance department still working on completing last month's financials, into the 3rd week of the month, you likely have at least one of these issues:

- Insufficient staffing in your finance department.
- Insufficient leadership in your finance function.
- Financial statements do not hold importance to senior management.

- Computer systems have not been modernized and, thus, finance staff does a lot of data stacking to get to the financial results.

Flash Sales

Most activity in a company is usually fairly consistent to historical patterns, except for sales. This is because there are many variables to how well the company performs in a given month, ranging from promotions, activities of the sales force, and competition in the economy in general. Accordingly, senior management is always extremely anxious to know the month's sales as soon as possible. This desire for quick reporting typically creates what is referred to as *flash sales*. The term, *flash sales*, is meant to say these are the first draft of the sales reporting, but the finance department has not finished the work to ensure that they are 100% accurate. Senior management typically recognizes that this is just the accountant's way of hedging their bets, and believes that the sales are usually 99% accurate; and that's more than adequate for senior management. Therefore, any well-run finance department produces a flash sales report on the very first day of the month, which is eagerly read by senior management. Accountants then go off and do their various processes to ensure the data is accurate. Usually, on day 2, after the month end, they will produce the final detailed sales report.

In the event that there was a significant difference between the final actual sales reporting and the flash sales, the finance team will be required to investigate and provide a thorough explanation. If there is such an occurrence, it has usually arisen because of system issues, which create erroneous reporting. It is fair to say that in most companies this is not an issue, and the flash sales are in fact almost identical to the actual sales

Content of Monthly Financial Statements

There is no one type of financial report beyond the basics of an income statement, balance sheet, and cash flow statement. Once we get beyond these three standard financial reports, each business, regardless if public or private, will create reports that are meaningful to its management, which is usually a product of management's experiences and the industry in which it operates. The type of business—retailer, service, manufacturer, distributor, wholesaler—will also have a large impact on the reporting.

Here is a typical format of an income statement, which summarizes a business:

- Sales
- Cost of Sales
- Gross Margin
- Expenses:
    - Selling
    - Marketing
    - Administrative
    - Operations
    - Regulatory
    - Interest

- Depreciation/Amortization
- Non-Operating
- Total Expenses
- Net Income Before Tax
- Income Taxes
- Net Income After Tax

Depending on which type of business, there will be much more detailed reporting on the key areas of the income statement for that type of business.

In retail, the sales line will receive the most focus. Sales will be split into:

- Gross sales
- Discounts from in-store promotions
- Discounts by vendors' coupons
- Discounts from product sold below normal selling price
- Net sales

This level of detail would be done for each physical location, and then there would be comparisons between each location on a monthly, YTD, prior YTD, and budget basis. Where one location is doing better than others, it would serve as a model for the others. Where one location is doing the worst, management would be studying this operation much more closely to understand the unfavourable performance, and creating action plans for improvement. Retail has the benefit, compared to other types of business, where you interact directly with the consumer.

If there are good sales reporting systems, then trends are known quickly, as any retail business is open for business every day, and must be making sales to the same levels as in prior periods to continue to exist and prosper.

In service businesses, the key ingredient to financial success is the cost of inputs, and what revenue they created. Typically, in a professional business, like accounting, law, engineering, or computer consultation, the business charges out its staff at an hourly rate, which can be 2.5x or even 3x as much as the actual cost of that employee. Accordingly, the key determination of success are issues like:

What is the utilization rate for each employee? That is, if there are 40 hours in a week * 52 weeks = 2,080 hours in the normal work year. What % of this total does each employee bill out to a client? Depending on the policies about overtime, it may be expected that each top performing employee has a 100% utilization rate; in other words, that they bill out 2,080 hours a year. This means they probably work about 2,300 to 2,400 hours a year, to allow for non-billable time and vacations.

What is the collectable rate for each employee? Even if an employee is billing out 100% of their time, do the clients pay for it all? The employee may be putting in the time, but effectiveness, in the view of the client, may be different than the firm. Thus, some of the billed time may be required to be written off. This becomes another standard: what % of the billable hours are collected?

Regardless of evaluating individual performers, a company needs to establish its overall company rate to ensure its success. This will have been done during the budget process, and will have been based on past performance. As an example, the budget may set the standard that the total wages * 2.5 should equal total revenue. If this is not happening, then there will be variance analysis by department, and by employee, to see where the unfavourable performance has occurred, and thus corrective action will be needed.

In manufacturing, the key component of the income statement that requires scrutiny is the cost of sales. There will be, in any good manufacturer, a standard cost system to determine the cost of each good manufactured. Manufacturing is not an exact process each time versus the standards. Thus, there will be variances of labour, material, and overhead in the actual manufacturing process versus the standards established. These will be analysed in infinite detail each month to determine the causes of any unfavourable activities, which will require immediate corrective action so as to not continue this unfavourable performance.

In both distribution and wholesale businesses, the goods sold are bought at price x and sold at price y. This difference is the unit margin and, depending on the industry, there is a lot of variability of its size. As an example, the food industry operates, in many product categories, with less than a 5% gross margin, but makes its money via the large volumes. In contrast, distributors of consumer-type goods can easily be earning 50–

70% gross margins, and thus have opportunities for price cutting to still sell goods profitably but get them out of inventory. The key analysis here will be on a product-by-product and category-by-category basis, to compare gross margins for the current month, YTD, prior YTD, and versus budget. Where there is a significant variance in any of these period comparisons, there will need to be much further analysis to pinpoint the cause and determine correction action if possible. Unlike some of the other types of companies, a distributor or wholesaler may have consciously marked down a price to just sell off inventory and then not buy the product again. There may even be a loss to at least recover as much as possible of the inventory investment, and then not repeat this purchase. The key in this type of business is to ensure your inventory is sold off according to the time frame of the product's life cycle. If it is perishable, then it must be sold before the *best by* date. If it is a seasonal product, then it must be sold before the season is over; otherwise, you will have to hold it in inventory until the next season, or drastically discount it to just get rid of at the best price you can realize.

Analysis

The term, *analysis*, refers to digging deeper into the numbers, and providing more thorough explanation of what they mean. This can be as simple as just saying that you spent $10,000 in computer costs, and thus providing a list of the supplier invoices that describe the service on each invoice, with the amount and the list totals. More sophisticated analysis begins when there is a comparison between two numbers; for example, the actual results versus the budget. The analysis involves understanding the amounts in both categories and then comparing each, and identifying what is different between the two of them. Companies also do interim forecasts, which conceptually are the same as a budget, except they may be for different times (monthly, quarterly, semi-annually), but they still, ultimately, are a set of financial reports, and management wants to know how they're doing versus that set of reports.

The fundamental reasons why a good finance department will have a short, monthly financial close calendar is to allow for the time, after producing the financial statements, to do analysis. This is where finance professionals provide one of their best values, to identify activities in the business for senior management to act upon. These, by their nature, are not self-evident from the typical financial statements and, therefore, require more in-depth review of both the actual results versus the expectations and understanding of either the good performance or the bad, and how to continue on the right path.

There are also analyses that are repetitive by nature, because it is required every month. Such an analysis then just becomes another set of financial reporting after the monthly financial statements are complete. The most value-added analysis is ad-hoc, where a finance professional identifies unusual trends or unusual results, delves into the numbers to better understand what is going on, and provides management with his/her feedback so they can take appropriate action.

Involvement of Non-Financial Management

A good finance department recognizes itself as a service department. What is the service? It is providing financial information to management. The most effective finance departments are those that work with the non-financial management team in providing this service, having a discussion about the information provided, and operating in a give-and-take style to see what it means and what further can be investigated to in fact provide even better information. This presumes that the non-financial manager personnel are well versed in the financial results of their given area, and that they can provide insights to the finance team to better understand the information so that finance has a better direction of how to do further analysis.

In my experience, where I've seen the most effective finance team, it is the one that works hand-in-hand with the non-financial team, to understand the numbers and jointly decide on investigations to be done for the better operation of the company. I have also seen where the non-financial manager disregards the finance team and just sees them as a bunch of number crunchers providing factual information. Thus, they do not engage with them to provide the operational insights that the finance team needs to better investigate the results. These are typically companies that are operating in silos and, therefore, do not enjoy the benefits of cross team effectiveness.

Public Reporting

For external reporting, there are statutory requirements that set more than a minimum standard for reporting. Aside from filing the reports that are required by the stock exchange with which the company is registered, most public companies will have some type of public media announcement of the results of the latest period. The most used method today is a webinar or public conference call, where the company management presents the latest results, comments on them, and provides explanations about the results, and there may or may not be time provided for questions from the audience. The audience consists of shareholders and any industry financial analysts who follow the company.

I have found that beyond providing the fundamental financial statements, public company analysis is more focused on explanation of variances, whereas private companies are more action-orientated and, thus, want deeper analysis, which identifies the root causes of unusual results so that corrective action can be taken.

Reporting/Presentation of Financial Statements in a Private Company

The presentation of the monthly financial statements to senior management is the best time for the CFO to be involved in the business. It is best that such a presentation be part of the normal monthly scheduled calendar so that the CFO knows that he/she will have the eyes and ears of senior management on a regular basis.

In my experience, beyond presenting the numbers, such a meeting delves into discussions about the business and where it is or is not performing well. This provides great opportunities for the CFO and the finance department to contribute to the improvement of the business. It should be obvious, but I am going to state anyway that at such a meeting, the CFO needs to be well versed in all aspects of the financial report for that month, so that he/she is able to answer any questions from senior management. The best part of such a meeting is that unusual results from the operational senior management perspective become evident and provide further potential opportunities for the finance department to do value-adding work. A top-notch finance department sees itself as a service department, whose service is providing information, and it should relish the opportunity to be of service, since finance departments who do this are those that senior management most appreciate.

As per my point above about public companies, I see this as the fundamental differentiation between a private and a public company. Public companies are most concerned with reporting externally and, therefore, all the numbers making sense, whereas a private company, typically, is most concerned with always improving. My own experience is that I have a much greater appreciation to be working on improvements rather than just reporting.

In the next chapter, I introduce the concept of *management's dashboard*. This is the quick scorecard that management wants to see quickly for the immediate feedback about the business.

Chapter Highlights

- Explaining the monthly close process, the activities involved, and proper timing.
- The difference between flash sales and actual sales, and why flash sales exist.
- The format is shown of what a typical income statement is.
- Discussion about the key differences in the focus of the income statement, depending on the type of business: retailer, service, manufacturer, distributor.
- Analysis is the best value-add activity a finance department can provide. This is where good finance departments devote their time, and it is so important to have a quick month- end close so that the maximum time is available for analysis. There are many types of analysis. Thus, the amount of time available, and the sophistication of your finance department, will determine how much value-add they provide.
- Non-finance managers decide the type of finance department they prefer: a value-adding group, or just a bunch of bean counters.
- One of the key differences between public and private companies is that public companies focus more on explaining variances, whereas private companies seek to truly make their operation as effective as possible.
- CFOs can have the most impact when they meet with the senior management and engage in in-depth discussion about unusual activities/results in the business, which provides opportunity for further analysis.

Chapter 5 – What Gets Measured, Gets Done

Highlights – Dashboard, KPIs

- What is a dashboard and KPIs?
- Target audience
- Format
- Establishing targets
- Example

What is a Dashboard and KPIs?

You will read in many places about metrics and KPI, but rarely do you find practical information and advice. In its simplest terms, metrics and KPI are standard pieces of information that are reported on a regular basis (hourly, daily, weekly, monthly, quarterly, annually). The time frame for reporting depends on the information and what frequency makes sense to use the information. As an example, in retail, you want to know your customer count, probably every hour. Looking at this information, at the end of each day, probably doesn't tell you much, because the first point of analysis would be to create trending information to see what hours of the day attract the most and least customers. To do this, you must have more than one day's data point to make comparisons. As a minimum, you would likely look at a week, and then be able to compare the same hour with 7 data points (7 days), and see whether it is the time of day or the week of the day that causes a change. You would likely be charting all 7 days, with all hours of the day, and this would be even more useful when done for many weeks (see the latest trend), for many months, so you can start seeing a long-term trending, even compared to the same week of one or two years ago. My point is very simple: Many businesses will tell you that business is down, and this may be just their sales, but they really don't know much else. Why? Because they are not doing KPI. If you, as a retailer, were tracking customer counts daily, by the 2nd week, you would know whether business was down as a trending statement and not just because sales were down. Now, you can take action, once you know specifically that there are less customers to create promotions against that time zone. For instance, if your sales are poor in the morning, maybe you need some door crasher sales, with limited quantities available. If late-day sales are down, then do a promotion that appeals to people as they are coming home from work (e.g., If you sell food—grocery or take out—perhaps you can create a package of food that is relevant for their dinner that night.).

Target Audience

The importance of metrics and KPI is simple: Measure that which you believe you can improve upon in your business if you knew. If you are collecting a bunch of statistics but can't make any impact on what they represent, then why collect them?

The most effective metrics and KPIs are those that are easy to track and stimulate action to change the result seen so far. Therefore, the target audience for KPIs or metrics is typically the owner and/or C-suite executives, because these are the people who have both the responsibility to manage the business and to most likely take action.

How many times have you talked to an entrepreneur who has created some rule of thumb guideline that they look for about their business, and when it is not being achieved, they already know they have some changes in their business that they must respond to? They don't wait to hear from their accountants, nor their marketing gurus; they already know there is an issue, and they are taking action. These are the KPIs that you want for your business. This just becomes a method of delegation from the owner/manager to his/her team, so that the team can take action that the owner /manager would have taken just because of his/her innate knowledge of his/her business, whereas the team has to look for systems to tell them. Some of us would call this experience. Well, few people in a business have the experience of the owner/ manager and, thus, they must look for other means to substitute this experience. That's where metrics and KPIs come in. No matter the size of the business, someone more experienced would spot the issue, but you, with less knowledge about the business, need a system of reporting to tell you these things. Over time, you will probably know the KPIs intuitively, and you will see the results immediately without the reports. The real importance of KPIs is to get you to focus on the issues that are important to your business.

Format

There is no magic format for KPIs or metrics. Every business, industry, and ownership is different. Therefore, what is useful for one, accomplishes nothing for another. The fundamental usefulness of a KPI or metric is that it provides information that the owner or C-suite team recognize as an important change in the business that requires action.

Therefore, it is not so much about the format as it is about what information is to be provided in KPIs and metrics. The most important part about KPIs and metrics is the timeliness of the information. This means that whatever information you have decided to report, is preferably produced by your normal reporting system. Sometimes information is deemed as being so important that manual preparation is necessary to get the information to the owner and/or C-suite executive. This is not the most desirable; however, if you've determined it is most important, then it's the right action.

These are the typical areas where most businesses will have KPIs and metrics:

- Sales dollars
- Number of customers and new customers added
- Sales per customer
- Top 10 customers, their history, and what % of total sales they are providing
- Inventory turnover
- Sales $ per employee
- Sales dollar per square foot for a retail store
- Customer traffic, usually by the hour
- Customer visits versus actual number of purchases
- Daily cash flow (see example on next page)
- Accounts receivable percentage past due
- Headcount

When it comes to format, again there is no prescribed rule. The method of presenting the information is typically tailored to the audience receiving it. Some executives prefer charts with a bunch of numbers; others like to see graphs and/or pie charts; still others prefer only to see the exceptions of the data that fall outside of a certain range of acceptability. My best advice is that once a KPI and metric reporting package has been prepared, it should be reviewed thoroughly with the owner and/or C-suite executive, for their input. Unfortunately, executives seem to be very meticulous on KPI and metrics, both in terms of data and format, notwithstanding my earlier comments. It can become very frustrating for the staff positions who are preparing the data to go back and forth many times until those executives are satisfied. The only way to minimize this is to engage the owner and/or C-suite executive at the beginning of the process, and review the reporting package closely with them.

Establishing Targets

In the past, most metrics and KPI came from the financial reporting system. The limitation with that is that most financial information, no matter how sophisticated your reporting system is—historical and really historical—it can be 35, 45, or even 60 days when that particular economic event has transpired. Too much time has likely elapsed to have any impact on what the data represents, and by the time you now implement something, it could be another 30 days, so the consumer behavior, which may have been a one-time transaction, has little meaning to the business so much after the fact.

Where do the targets come from for your KPIs and metrics? Typically, from your budget process. Once you have established a reporting regime of KPIs and metrics, it becomes just an add-on process to your budget routine. A lot of data picked for KPIs and metrics are not a clear data point in a financial reporting system. Some of the data is there, and then it may need a calculation to produce a metric. As an example, let's say you want to know the number of sales $ per employee. Your financial reporting system will, of course, have the sales dollars, and it may even have a separate database with a number of employees, although less likely. Then, of course, there is the actual calculation of taking the sales dollar divided by the number of employees, to arrive at the sales dollars per employee. If this were a KPI, then the preparation would likely fall to a member of the finance staff. Although this example is simple, it is understandable that the best KPIs are those that are automatically generated out of your normal reporting system. This is particularly true for any KPI that is to be reported on a daily basis. You don't want the C-suite executive running to the finance staff every day, asking where their KPIs are. You want an automated report that in fact is on their desk at 7AM, or in their email, so they can start the day having seen whatever they deem as being important to running your business.

One of the key issues for effective KPI is the timing for which they are reported. Every single KPI and metric could be, in theory, reported on a daily basis. The reality, though, is that daily reporting would not be useful and, therefore, it would be a waste of resources in its preparation. Therefore, the team responsible for KPI reporting, in conjunction with the C-suite executives, needs to determine the timing for each KPI, and whether it is part of the daily reporting package, weekly reporting package, or just once a month.

Example

Here is one example of an excellent KPI that both stimulates action and encapsulates many business fundamentals: the Daily Cash Flow Monitor Report. In its simplest format, here is what is recommended:

Day of the Month	Daily Receipts	Budget Receipts	Fav/ (Unfav)	Daily Spending	Budget Spending	Fav/ (Unfav)	Net Cash Flow – Actual	Net Cash Flow – Budget	Fav/ (Unfav)
1	450,000	500,000	(50,000)	450,000	450,000	0	0	50,000	(50,000)
2	475,000	500,000	(25,000)	450,000	450,000	0	25,000	50,000	(25,000)
3	525,000	500,000	25,000	450,000	450,000	0	75,000	50,000	25,000
4	550,000	500,000	50,000	450,000	450,000	0	100,000	50,000	50,000
5	400,000	500,000	(100,000)	450,000	450,000	0	(50,000)	50,000	(100,000)
6			0			0	0	0	0
7			0			0	0	0	0
8	400,000	500,000	(100,000)	400,000	450,000	50,000	0	50,000	(50,000)
9	475,000	500,000	(25,000)	400,000	450,000	50,000	75,000	50,000	25,000
10	450,000	500,000	(50,000)	400,000	450,000	50,000	50,000	50,000	0
11	425,000	500,000	(75,000)	400,000	450,000	50,000	25,000	50,000	(25,000)
12	440,000	500,000	(60,000)	400,000	450,000	50,000	40,000	50,000	(10,000)
Total	4,590,000	5,000,000	(410,000)	4,250,000	4,500,000	250,000	340,000	500,000	(160,000)

This report is done daily from the banking info. It is timely, as it should be on the desk of all executives by 10AM each day. It provides a quick overview of both the revenue and disbursement sides of the business. It gives feedback on all key aspects of the business:

- Sales (If you are not selling, then your collections will be lower.)
- Collections – Are you collecting what you sell?
- Disbursements – Is your spending in line with your sales and your plan?

- Net Cash – Are you only spending what you collect, and holding back if you create negative cash flow?

This is an example that has universal application. Every business needs to review what is important to them, and create the appropriate reporting, both in terms of content and timing, to report on those issues.

Financial statements are historical information with the actual results. In the next chapter, I introduce the more sophisticated area of future financial information: forecasts and budgets.

Chapter Highlights

- Dashboard or KPI information, to be effective, must be reported on in a long enough period that allows for trending of the data.
- KPIs need to be formatted to be meaningful to the audience targeted. The same data doesn't provide the same level of information to different groups of people, based on their knowledge of the business.
- Every industry has different KPIs that are meaningful and relevant to their senior management. The most important aspect of KPIs is to report them quickly so that the data is not stale, as KPIs are meant to provide possible red flags to senior management before issues/problems become severe.
- KPIs, to be effective, need to be reported timely, and wherever possible, be produced from the normal reporting system. Manual KPIs usually fall into disuse, since they are prone to human error, both in preparation and timeliness.

Chapter 6 – Managing Your Business with Financial Tools

Budgeting and Income Statement Forecasting

- Overview
- Objective
- Schedule
- Responsibilities
- Content
- Process
- Upside/downside
- End Result

Overview

The financial budget is typically the estimate of the next year's financial statement. The budget is a document that portrays the business planning, but it is stated in financial terms. The level of detail for which the budget is prepared will be done in direct proportion to the level of detail that a company wishes to report its monthly internal financial statements. Typically, there should be a budget for each income statement general ledger account, so that there is a standard set against which to measure the actual results for that general ledger account. However, if a budget manager responsible for a given area is only looking at totals, rather than an individual general ledger account, then preparing a budget to that level will just be a wasted exercise, with extra work that is not being used.

A financial forecast is similar to the financial budget, except it is typically done by the month or quarter, or even semi-annually. The purpose of a financial forecast is typically the updating of the budget. Each company will make its own determination of the level of detail of the financial forecast. It is preferable that the financial forecast be prepared to the same level as was done for the budget. In this way, it provides a perfect update to the budget. Many companies do not wish to expend the same level of resources in the preparation of a financial forecast as was done for a budget. The forecast may be in a much more summarized level. The importance of a financial forecast is as an update to management, with more recent information about the overall financial affairs of the company.

The main differences between the budget and financial forecast are time periods represented. Beyond this, the differences are slight. Therefore, the sections that follow combine the discussion around the budget and financial forecast in each of the top headings. I use the acronym, B/FF, to mean budget/financial forecast.

Objective

When a company embarks on its B/FF, management must decide what the purpose is of the exercise. Is it purely a numbers exercise to put into your reporting system B/FF data, so that there is comparison to the actual results? Is it done as part of the strategic planning process to translate strategies into numbers? Is it part of a three to five-year business planning process, or just a one-year exercise? In simple terms, management must decide why it is doing this exercise.

There's no question that having a B/FF sets an objective target for where the company wants to see its results. It isn't easy, but it is the main system for better monitoring of the monthly results. These reasons, by themselves, are sufficient to go through the exercise of doing a B/FF. Then there's the added team development aspect of budgeting, where teams work together on it, and there is a synergy created of the entire team getting behind the achievement, which has spin-off motivational aspects. The B/FF may also be the proper resource allocation exercise of both money and people towards the company objectives.

Schedule

The B/FF schedule, in simple terms, is a listing of the tasks to be done, by who, and by what date. It should be appointed to a BPM (budget project manager) who has the responsibility for coordinating all facets of the budget to all the responsible parties. This person would prepare the initial schedule and present it to all the people involved in the preparation of the B/FF. It is advisable to hold a pre-budget meeting for all staff involved in the preparation of the B/FF. The BPM would present the schedule, explain each activity, and get buy-in from the responsible party for the completion of each task in the timeline shown on the schedule.

The B/FF schedule is a sequential activity, where step 2 is reliant on Step 1, and step 3 is reliant on Step 2, etc. This means that if one of the steps is late, all the other steps would likely be delayed. Therefore, it is essential that there is agreement among the participants on the timing of when tasks are completed. That is why it is extremely advisable to have the pre-B/FF meeting well in advance of the start of the process, to gain the buy-in of all the participants. It is also advisable that if any participant reluctantly accepts the timeline in the schedule, if possible, that task should be moved back to a date for which the participant is more confident of meeting the deadline.

B/FF preparation involves many participants and, therefore, is a team exercise. It is extremely de-motivating for those participants who prepare their work on time, only to be held back by 1 or 2 participants who are late. This also means that the BPM needs to be constantly monitoring the performance and completion of the tasks by all participants, and follow-up as required to keep the schedule on time. One further aspect of the schedule that should be obvious, but I will highlight it here, is that aside from the tasks, there are meetings scheduled relying on certain tasks being done. If a task is delayed, it likely causes a subsequent meeting to be rescheduled. This becomes extremely difficult to do so if many people are expected to attend such a meeting.

Responsibilities

Just listing the names of the individuals that are responsible for task X, is insufficient. The BPM needs to review with each individual what the tasks on the schedule mean, in full detail, and ensure buy-in. It is usually wise for the BPM to actually produce the format of the reporting required in the budget; otherwise, he/she will likely not get what he/she expects. Similarly, if an entire department is responsible for a certain activity, the BPM needs to meet the head of the department and gain agreement for specific people responsible for specific activities.

It is not desirable to produce a long list of memos so that everything is documented as a *cya* activity. However, providing written directions is an excellent way to leave each individual with the agreed upon assignment so that they can go back and refresh for themselves, whenever they need to, so that they continue preparing what was agreed upon. Lack of written directions will usually result in the individuals not following through correctly with the instructions, because they forget. Therefore, it is not only proven but also effective to prepare B/FF instructions in writing, and to the level of detail of showing the final end product.

Content

Using an income statement outline as the ultimate format required for a B/FF, here are the details for each of these items in terms of what is required to be prepared.

Sales

The amount of sales is the aggregate of the number of units * the selling price for each product. This is a good example where management must decide the extent of work to be done. If the budget is done at a SKU level, and depending on how many SKUs each company has, it can create a very extensive time preparation for this task. The alternative would be to budget on the basis of categories and growth rates.

Cost of Sales

The cost of sales cannot be determined until sales are determined. Depending on whether sales are determined by SKU or by category, will then follow suit in the determination of cost of sales. Cost of sales is then either the unit cost * the number of units, or a percentage of sales dollars.

Expenses

These are the typical expense categories:

- Selling expense
- Marketing expense
- Office administration and overhead
- Operations expense
- Regulatory expense
- Interest cost
- Non-Operating Expense

In each of these categories, there will be a list of general ledger accounts that make up the category. Detailed budgeting would be done by determining the amount for each general ledger account. Details would typically be based on the prior-year actual, after reviewing the details of the actuals and making new assumptions about what is going to change. There are some categories where a general rate of increase is used to make the determination of the budget amount. When there are very clear specifics that make up a general ledger account (listing of people and their wages as an example), the specifics are determined individually.

Process

The usual process of a budget is for each participant to submit to the BPM the items for which they are responsible. The BPM will review their submission compared to the responsibilities list and suggested reporting, and ensure that it complies with schedule, both in terms of timing and content. The BPM is usually tasked with the role of accumulating all the information submitted, and ultimately preparing a budget package for management. The budget package will summarize the submissions in an easy to read, time-effective manner for management.

In those cases where participants' submission does not comply with the original schedule, the BPM needs to review this with the participant and get them to make whatever adjustments are necessary to do so. This needs to be done while keeping the process on schedule. Again, to reiterate, any delays in any of the tasks can cause meetings scheduled to be rescheduled, which is usually problematic since everyone usually has many competing priorities.

Depending on the company and the desire of senior management of how many people should be involved in the budget presentation, will dictate how many people actually attend the meeting where the budget is presented. Usually, there's one of two ways to go:

a. Each budget manager presents their area.
b. The budget project manager presents the entire budget, and calls upon budget managers as necessary.

Item (a) is an all-inclusive process, which certainly yields better buy-in by all participants. However, it is much more time-consuming for all participants and management, because many more people are involved, and there are typically more presentations made, and more discussion is held, along with the complexity of co-ordinating the schedules of many people.

Item (b) has the advantage of keeping meetings shorter, and more streamlined and focused on the main presentation. There is always the option to call upon individual budget managers to explain specific items, and giving management that option is necessary, but it limits the amount of preparation and time commitment by individual budget managers.

Regardless of whether (a) or (b) is chosen, after the meeting, there needs to be follow-up on all of the questions raised, and actions to be taken by the team, so that the entire cycle of the budget process can be completed. This is typically an area that is a weak point in many companies. A large part of the reason is that the outcome of the meetings is not something that can be scripted in advance. Sometimes questions or comments are unclear, and this creates uncertainty of the action required. In the meantime, there was no schedule established, or responsibility for when items were to be done, or for their format and completion. The main point that I want to emphasize is that the BPM must take control of the process, document the outcome of the meeting, and follow up diligently with all parties until all activities are completed.

Upside/Downside

One of the best tools I have seen in B/FF preparation has been called the upside/downside analysis. Given that the B/FF is basically a financial prediction, this means that there are assumptions made in the process. Any assumption has a degree of uncertainty (If there were no uncertainty, then it would not be an assumption.). Examples of assumptions:

- We will sign a new customer, who will add 5% to our sales.
- We will launch these new products, which will add 3% to our sales, and these new products will be launched at the midpoint of the year.
- We will lose the distribution agreement with company X, which will cause 2% lost sales starting in month 4 of the year.
- We will create a new position—national sales manager—for which someone will be hired at the start of the year, which will cost $x and deliver $x of added sales.

The purpose of the upside/downside analysis is to highlight for senior management where the soft spots are (the assumptions, both good and bad) that may be too optimistic or pessimistic, so that senior management can better assess the likelihood of the outcome expected by the budget manager for that area. This typically stimulates a much more strategic discussion on the reasons and expectations for this given activity.

The upside/downside analysis is actually two pages: one for upsides, and one for downsides. Each will list the key components of each activity for:

- Sales
- Cost of sales
- Expenses
- Assumed start date for the activity
- Brief description of the activity
- Expectation of the financial amounts coming to fruition, stated as a % probability

In my experience, the simple rule of thumb is that anything with a 50% or greater expectation of realization is included in the B/FF, and anything below 50% stays listed on the upside/downside sheets. Therefore, the upside/downside serves as a catalyst to decide which new possible activities are approved to be put in the B/FF.

End Result

As a minimum, the end result of the budget process should be these documents:

a. Sales by category or SKU
b. Cost of sales by category or SKU
c. Expense amount for each expense category (possibly with amounts for each general ledger account)
d. Budgeted income statement

f. A headcount budget by person, and their estimated compensation
g. List of assumptions made in the preparation of the budget
h. Upside/downside analysis
i. Any key decisions made by management
j. Any follow-up actions that are not reflected in the budget

The data from items a, b, c, and d is entered into your reporting system so that it is available to be compared to the actual results on a monthly and YTD basis.

This chapter has outlined financial forecasting. The next chapter introduces operational sales forecasts, which are fundamental to meeting customer requirements.

Chapter Highlights

- A budget or financial forecast should be the financial presentation of the business plan. The amount of time and effort spent will be directly proportional to the extent of work done on business planning. Aside from its obvious capability of setting a budget or financial forecast, it can provide a great team building exercise to all departments aligned around the company's objectives.

- The budget or financial forecast is a sequential process of building data and/or assumptions at each step, and the steps in the later stage of the process rely on the earlier data or assumptions. Thus, it is essential that timelines are met throughout the process for its effective preparation.

- The budget or financial forecast process can be a very involved process, with all departments involved (both finance and non-finance), or can be directed by finance, with involvement of non-finance, on an as-needed basis. There is no perfect system. It is very much dependent on the culture of the company and the amount of time and resources that senior management wants to spend on this activity.

- The upside/downside report is one of the best vehicles to stimulate strategic discussion about the business.

- A listing is provided of the likely reports contained in a budget or financial forecast reporting package.

Chapter 7 – Using Financial Tools in All Areas of the Business

Sales Forecasts and Inventory Planning

- Process
- Sales forecasting
- Inventory purchasing
- Accuracy and targets
- Corrective action

Process

Are you able and ready to fully meet your customer's desires for your products? In this section, I am focusing on customers who have decided to buy your product, and the discussion is concentrated on finished goods that are ready for sale. There are two key questions:

- Do you have a reliable, consistent method to predict what your customer buys?
- Do you have the product the customer seeks when they are ready to make a purchase?

The process to predict the product that you think your customer desires is called sales forecasting. In its simplest terms, it is your prediction, by product, of what quantity your customer will buy of each of your products. In order to do sales forecasting, a company typically involves representatives from the sales function and marketing. Sales professionals are those people in constant contact with customers. Therefore, they are the best people in your organization to understand customer behavior. Marketing staff prepare programs to stimulate the sales of your product. Therefore, a monthly meeting is usually the preferred method, where a representative of sales, marketing, and operations meet to review the monthly sales forecast. This meeting is usually referred to as the *Demand Forecast Meeting*. The fundamental goal of the Demand Forecast Meeting is to make sure that each of these functional areas is well aware of external issues with customers, and internal issues with product and inventory, to make the correct determinations of the sales forecast. These meetings do not need to be a long drawn-out affair. Rather, it is the discipline of constant monthly monitoring and adjusting to keep on top of customer behavior as reflected in the products they are buying.

Once the quantity of each product you think you will sell is determined, then a decision needs to be made of how much inventory will be stocked to meet that demand. This is typically a role handled by operations staff, and can be done in isolation by them or in conjunction with the sales and marketing team. In the section below, titled *Inventory Purchasing*, all the various parameters that need to be considered are outlined. As it relates to the process, the same meaning that is used for the sales forecasting process can also incorporate considerations about inventory purchasing. It is best for there to be discussion amongst sales, marketing, and operations in consideration of all the various parameters for inventory purchasing, to ensure that any unusual circumstances are considered and discussed.

Sales Forecasting

This is the system to attempt to predict which products will be bought, and in what quantities, by your customers. This is essential for any well-run operation to be close enough to its business to have a database of information of past customer purchases, which are combined with a reliable method of prediction, to make estimates of future customer purchases. These estimates are known as forecasts, and are used as the basis to order the inventory that you will stock, and in what quantities.

The system needs to incorporate these components:

- A robust computerized system that tracks each SKU (Stock Keeping Unit) purchase and sales history by date, so that it can be displayed in monthly data charts. These charts are available in report form or graphic design, as preferred by management, as well as the operational staff who are working with this daily.
- Your system should have mathematical formulae that can predict future customer sales based on past purchases.
- Your staff should be competent to use and understand these mathematical formulae to assess the likelihood of these predications, and what changes, if any, should be made before inventory is ordered/produced.
- Your staff needs to be sophisticated enough to factor in how the customer purchases will change when there are retail incentives offered, both from past history and just general marketing knowledge about your customer.

Typically, this forecasting function is fulfilled by marketing staff who are at a head office or corporate level, as this type of activity should be centralized to gain economies of scale for the operation.

This forecasting function is typically done monthly, shortly after the previous month's actual results are known. The forecast period, depending on procurement timetables, is 3–6 months in advance.

Inventory Purchasing

The purchase of inventory is determined by the sales forecast as described above. Purchase/procurement staff take the sales forecast and negotiate with suppliers (where they are buying finished goods) the best price possible for the quantities that you wish to buy. Usually, the price is negotiated at the beginning of the year (can be calendar year or fiscal year of supplier, or fiscal year of buying company), and then remains the same for all purchases during the year.

An effective purchaser will seek incentives for buying more than a pre-set amount or the prior year's sales. Sometimes the purchasing company has a special activity planned for which it seeks some type of assistance from the supplier to then offer better deals to its customers. This can take the form of a lower price or financial assistance, with the advertising done by the buying company. This is known as co-operative advertising, and the supplier will get space in the advertising medium used by the purchasing company, which of course becomes a win/win for both parties. The supplier pays a portion of the advertising, but the unit pricing is very economical, and the buying company has done all the work to produce it, as well as communicate this info to its entire customer data base. Effectively, the supplier has bought time/space from the buying company to communicate with the buying company's customers.

Companies establish financial/operational guidelines of how much inventory they will stock of each SKU. In other words, based on the sales forecast, a purchaser is buying the amount of inventory that will position the company to have, for example, 60 days of inventory in stock. This means that based on the sales prediction, there is enough inventory on hand that will last for 60 days if the sales occur as predicted. The determination of whether the target should be 45, or 60 or 75, is dependent on a number of factors:

Customer service culture: You always want to have stock. *Stock outs* are an unacceptable result to be presented to your customer (i.e. in the retail business, an empty shelf). Many companies will establish a backorder policy as to what quantity of backorder is tolerated, and for how long. The lower the backorder target, the higher the inventory needs to be to avoid this low back order.

What is the lead time to order your next round of inventory? The higher the lead time, the higher your inventory needs to be, as you have longer periods to wait for your next order.

The accuracy of your sales forecast system, based on your past track record, will determine your confidence level of how much safety stock you need to create in your inventory.

Is there any uniqueness to a product? The more unique, the more reliant you are on the supplier, and they may be on backorder, versus a product where you can procure it from a number of different suppliers, or in a very short period.

Reliability of your supplier is a critical aspect of how much inventory you stock of their product.

Company's financial strength: The more capital available, the more that can be invested in inventory. Companies that are struggling, typically minimize their inventory, either by having less of the products that have a quick ability to re-order, or minimal stock of slow-moving items. These are typically financial prudent decisions, provided they are not so low to create a strong likelihood of running out of stock before it can be replaced.

Products that are special order because they are customer specific, by definition, are not stocked in inventory.

The above process relates to the purchase of finished goods inventory, and not manufactured product that you manufacture.

Accuracy and Targets

Another aspect of the Demand Forecast Meeting is to review the accuracy of the sales forecasting. Each month, the team should be looking at the actual sales results versus the prior forecast. In this way, the team is constantly evolving the sales forecast, based on customer feedback, through the actual sales performance. In the short term, a month or two, it is unlikely that variances in sales performance versus forecast will be clearly understood to make significant changes to the future sales forecast. However, that is the very reason that the team is meeting to discuss the results and jointly decide on whatever changes are deemed appropriate for the sales forecast. A good operations team will quantify the accuracy of the sales forecasting every month and, therefore, be able to highlight the specific SKUs where the accuracy is unsatisfactory. Of course, the level of accuracy acceptable needs to be predetermined as a standard for the company.

In regard to those products where the sales accuracy is proving to be unsatisfactory, the team needs to have an action plan of determining the reason for said inaccuracy. This may involve analysis by sales and marketing personnel, and/or having the sales staff actually talk to customers to do some mini surveying. The fundamental issue is the constant monitoring of your customers' behavior as reflected in the actual sales performance

Corrective Action

Inaccurate sales forecasting, for whatever reason, is just one aspect of unsatisfactory inventory management. As discussed in the preceding section, the team, by virtue of monthly monitoring results and investigating unusual variances to the forecasting, should be taking ongoing actions to correct the sales forecast. There are many fundamental considerations made on the product procurement side, as described in the section above on inventory purchasing. Although many of these are more of a strategic decision, that by itself does not make them immune from constant review. As an example, it may have been decided that product X should always have 60 days in inventory. This may have been done in the past because of a long lead time, and/or it had a high volatility in its sales performance. If the circumstances around this product X have changed in any of these aspects, then the past decision of stocking 60 days of inventory should be reviewed. Therefore, each one of the inventory principles should be susceptible to constant review in the Demand Forecast Meeting. Stated more bluntly, there should be no sacred cows. In the past, as an example, a 99% service level may have been deemed to be necessary in our industry. That doesn't mean that we accept this as a principle forever. Circumstances change. Customers' expectations change. Therefore, these principles always need to be re-evaluated if they are not meeting the strategic direction of the business.

In the next chapter, I provide key issues about managing your team—Human Resources, practical processes, and payroll—as it affects employees.

Chapter Highlights

- Sales, marketing, and operations personnel should be meeting on a monthly basis to determine the sales forecast by SKU.
- The sales forecast should be a software program that, with the input of various assumptions, will provide a sales forecast for the next 3–6 months by SKU.
- Inventory purchases use the sales forecast as the amount of inventory that will be sold. There are a number of assumptions inherent in the inventory purchase strategy, such as how many days of inventory you are willing to hold in stock, or what period of time is acceptable to have a back order, which determines the quantity to be ordered.
- Sales forecasting is an estimating process; thus, it needs constant monitoring to understand when it is not accurate, and to determine what the causes are of inaccuracy. This is important to know, as the methodology may need to change.
- If it is determined that the methodology is yielding inaccurate results, either in the sales forecast methodology or in the inventory principles used to make purchases, these need to change to meet the changing circumstances.

Chapter 8 – Managing Your Team

HR, Managing Wages, Payroll

- HR related rights legislation
- Process for wages and changes
- Work performance reviews
- Employee handbook
- Selection of a payroll provider
- Canadian Payroll Association

HR Related Rights Legislation

In this day and age, the rights of the individual have come to surpass those of the collective group, be it society in general or a company. In the province of Ontario, we most recently had Bill 148, which is basically a human rights set of rules and regulations encoded into our labour regulations. The new Conservative government passed Bill 47, on November 21, 2018, repealing most of the socialistic style legislation. The reason this becomes important for companies is that Bill 148 codified an enforcement department to ensure that the rules established were in fact followed. This means there is a bureaucracy which, for businesses, becomes troublesome in terms of meeting compliance requirements. What does this all mean for you running a business? You need to make sure that your company is following the rules properly. If you don't, you run the risk of some government bureaucrat doing an audit and then initiating a fine for your company, and/or creating other compliance requirements that may be onerous.

Many times in this book, I will strongly recommend that you hire the proper expertise rather than expecting generalists in your HR or finance department to handle this. If you are to hire an HR consultant who has many clients, they are managing Bill 148 and Bill 47. Thus, they become an expert and, therefore, you gain the benefit of the learning curve already having been established, and your firm being the beneficiary. Not only will there be reporting requirements, but more importantly, there likely are policy changes, and even culture changes, for your firm. One of the fundamental areas, inherent in bill 148, was increasing the rights of the part-time worker. If your business has made extensive use of part-time work, you will absolutely want to be well-versed: How do you replace workers, and what changes do you need to make in your normal practice? The last thing you need is one employee who is outspoken and contacts the bureaucracy because they deem you are not following the rules. I can assure you that you will spend extensive time throughout your organization in the event of such an eventuality. Leaving aside the obvious that it is best to comply with the rules, the real point I want to make here is to hire the right expertise so that you implement the proper procedures in the first place, to likely avoid any of these types of problems.

The HR function is similar to the finance function, and has two fundamental areas of expertise: assisting management utilizes its human resource capital as best as possible, and complying with rules and reporting related to employees as required of the jurisdiction in which you operate. New legislation, like Bills 148 and 47, do create scenarios for your HR department that become extensive in terms of compliance. They should not be minimized in terms of the time that it takes for them, and is another reason that it is advisable to hire outside consultants to get this done properly.

Finance and HR generally share payroll related activities. There is no right answer as to whether the HR department or the finance department should be the actual custodian of the payroll records and their preparation. However, my opinion is that the

HR department is typically central to the managing of the wages of employees. Therefore, it is a better division of duties for the finance function to be the custodian of the preparation of the payroll. HR's interest in payroll is simply the factual records of what employees make. Finance's interest is for the proper recording of the wage and benefit cost into the financial records, and proper reporting to the various jurisdictions interested in your payroll information.

Process for Wages and Changes

The process of hiring an employee is the beginning point for a new employee to be on your payroll. Before you get to that point, however, it is wise to have a process for making the decision to add a new employee. The cost of every employee is more than just their salary or wage. Not only are there the obvious costs (costs of benefits), but there is the management time for somebody to be their boss and to have to manage them. Every organization would be wise to have a thorough process of reviewing their organizational structure, the positions in it, and the necessity for those positions. This should be done as part of the budget process every year. It is a good exercise for every department to justify to senior management the number of people in his/her department. This becomes an excellent way to ensure we are always looking for efficiencies in an organization, rather than just adding more people.

Once the decision has been made by senior management to add an employee, there should be a formal document that is processed to add that employee into the workforce. It will list the following:

- Start date
- Full employee name
- Employee address
- Spouse/partner name and contact info for emergency contact
- Social insurance number
- Date of birth
- Driver's license
- Car license
- Passport, if they have one
- Wage rate
- Benefits (vacation, car allowance, cell phone, computer, and any other perks of the job/company assets that they will have access to)
- Group benefit plan enrollment information

The employee information is then signed by the hiring manager and sent to the payroll department for inclusion of the new person on payroll.

Any time that any information on the employee record form changes, a new form should be prepared and marked for the changes. In this way, only the changes need to be recorded, and the same form can be used. Therefore, whether it's something as simple as an address change or a wage change, you may use the same form. Only information that affects the amount of money or benefits that the company is giving to the employee, should require the hiring manager to sign off on the form. Otherwise, the employee may just send the form with the changes directly to the payroll department.

Work Performance Reviews

Work performance reviews (WPR) is the phrase typically used for the evaluation, done by management, of an employee. Other than in a union environment, where the productivity or changes that will be allowed to be implemented are typically through contract negotiation, the WPR process is the best avenue to help an employee improve. The WPR is best used once a year, and not just for performance improvement but also as the proper basis to determine remuneration changes. Unlike a union environment, where an annual raise is something contracted regardless of performance, a WPR process ensures that employees are differentiated based on their performance. Nothing can generate better employee improvement than directly matching their performance with their pay.

Once an employee has been hired and has been put on payroll, the WPR process becomes the means by which any compensation changes should be made. In this way, it is an objective once-a- year review that should, if properly completed, yield the objective evidence of changes to be made in compensation. It is suggested that the WPR be done more frequently, but usually management has enough trouble doing it once per year. The reality is that most human beings are happy to give positive affirmation, but not negative, or requests for improvement. Unless the improvement is really severely required, then it is typical that it is just not done, and then, all of a sudden, at the end of the year, the WPR form is required. As an analogy, I've written about maintaining financial records on a daily basis, for transaction processing, is the right thing for the business. In a similar vein, doing the right thing for the employees means employees should be dealt with properly—both for the good and for the bad—so that the employee knows where they stand at the end of the year. Thus, by doing a WPR, there should be no surprises. The best way that I have found is to have an employee do a self WPR, and if the hiring manager and the employee do them independently, the discussion becomes a tremendous vehicle to make sure that they are in sync in their perspective. I have found that most employees will be tougher on themselves than their manager is, and they will rate themselves lower. This, then, provides the manager an easy opportunity to give them a pat on the back.

Employee Handbook

Once you have more than a handful of employees, it is wise to create an employee handbook. Given the difference in personal culture, age, and work experience, you want the culture of your company to be defined by you. This is done most effectively by having an employee handbook that outlines the company philosophy of how the business is run, how employees are treated, and the rules. This ensures that there are no misunderstandings. These are some typical areas covered in such a handbook:

- Company mission statement and history
- Confidentiality policy
- Code of conduct and ethics policy
- Equal opportunity policy
- Harassment policy
- Discipline rules and procedures
- Employee time off from work
- Attendance rules
- Workplace professional and company representation
- Travel and entertainment policy
- Safety and security
- Payroll info
- Benefits info
- Use of company equipment and other assets
- Performance expectations and evaluation

Selection of a Payroll Provider

The selection of a payroll processing company is no different than procurement decisions. There should be a set of criteria of what the company needs in a payroll processing company, and then you search out the various companies in this field who offer the services.

I have found, regardless of the area for which I am seeking a service, the best way for me to learn more about that given field is to meet with the various vendors in the field. I usually have already prepared my own selection criteria, and then, through discussion, learn more about what is going on in that sector, so that I can refine my requirements and ultimately choose the vendor best for the company's needs. In Canada, there are only a few major payroll processing companies, such as ADP and Ceridian. There are, of course, many self solutions, through software on the internet or the cloud (PAYweb, QuickBooks online, and Payworks). As I have stated earlier, the software from these various companies is adequate to do the job and prepare the payroll. The issue becomes the fact that the person selected within the company to perform the function may have minimal knowledge about it, and therefore can be prone to errors through lack of knowledge. Even the most knowledgeable, experienced payroll professional has a hard time these days to keep up to date with the changes in the rules, procedures, etc. Therefore, as a minimum, you should use payroll software for the preparation of your payroll, regardless of how small your firm is. This allows you to at least be using a product that should identify most of the issues. One of the other issues that is important is the compatibility of the payroll software with your accounting software. Can the payroll data be easily exported into your accounting software, with minimal effort by your finance department to restack the data? These are the types of questions you want to explore before you decide on your payroll provider.

Like many services that one requires, one of the best ways to determine your choice is to ask for the references, and actually really talk to the references. I certainly found that if you are prepared with a list of very specific questions, the reference will be happy to spend the 10 or 15 minutes to answer them, and you'll find out much more information this way than what you get out of the vendor.

Once you do make your selection, most of the companies are competent and know their field. The real issue becomes managing them on an ongoing basis, so that if there are misunderstandings, any mistakes are handled quickly and competently, and not allowed to fester. This is usually the source of major problems.

Payroll is normally seen as a junior activity within finance departments, yet nothing probably upsets employees more than something wrong with their paycheque. It is for that reason I strongly recommend you hire a professional payroll company, like ADP or Ceridian, for two key reasons:

- They are the experts in their field, and you are paying for this expertise to be up to date with all rules and regulations.
- If there are mistakes, companies like ADP or Ceridian, because of their knowledge, are more equipped to make corrections quickly, which goes a long way to soothe an upset employee.

Having a payroll company will ensure that annual activities, like the preparation of T4s (annual statement to each employee of how much they earned, to be filed with their tax return), reconciliation of the payroll reported to CRA vs the T4s, as well as Workman's Compensation filings and Employer Health Tax filings, are all balanced, paid, and complete. These are activities where each can take many hours, and if incomplete, will cause no end of extra work with the government agencies. Accordingly, you want it handled by professionals who take that compliance responsibility.

Canadian Payroll Association

If you choose to do your payroll by having a member of your finance department prepare the payroll and handle all the remittances, I strongly recommend that your firm join the Canadian Payroll Association (CPA). This is a professional services organization of people who have satisfied the certification process or are studying to gain the designation. Individuals and/or firms may join the CPA, which is a great resource for maintaining knowledge in the payroll field and having a resource to answer challenging issues in payroll. Their web site is https://www.payroll.ca.

The next chapter discusses the staffing you need in your finance department to provide all the reporting and information that has been discussed.

Chapter Highlights

- Business needs to be ever mindful when there are changes in government with a different political slant that likely causes the change of past rules and laws. This can have a major impact on a company and its normal operations. The right experts, who have many clients facing the changes, should be hired so that the company keeps its operations focused and is not distracted with governance issues.

- Headcount changes/additions are a major investment for most companies, and thus there should be a formal process for reviewing the entire headcount of the company. The best place to fulfill this activity, in my opinion, is as part of the budget process.

- A work performance review (WPR) is the activity done to review an employee's performance, usually annually. This is a great opportunity to give an employee positive feedback and be candid about areas of improvement.

- In our multicultural society, where there are different norms learned at home, it is critical for a company to spell out in an employee handbook the culture and rules of the company. This will save a lot of miscommunication and potential conflicts.

- Preparation of payroll can be done by a staff person in finance or HR. Given the constant changes in compensation legislation, I recommend you hire a payroll processing company to do the payroll, which will ensure you are always compliant.

- If you don't hire a payroll processing company, then as a minimum, be a member of the Payroll Association so that your staff has a place to get expertise.

Chapter 9 – The Effective Finance Team

How to Staff This Department

- Common traits in effective finance departments
- Typical positions in a finance department
- Role of the external accountant
- Managing the finance department

CommonTraits in Effective Finance Departments

I have had the good fortune of managing many finance professionals. The one common trait that I always see is the professionalism. Finance people are typically very dedicated and responsible. Perhaps it is in our DNA, as our role requires us to point out what others either want to ignore or just don't realize. The trick to having a top-notch finance department is to match the business needs with the person who has the best skills in your department to fulfill each responsibility.

I remember that after implementing a Shared Service Centre (SSC) in one company, I lobbied that we needed one person at the local level who would be the liaison person to the SSC. This person needed to be strong in accounting, to like accounting, and have a very easy-going nature to blend the local needs to be serviced by the SSC that was 3,000 miles away. Luckily, one of the local staff, who otherwise was going to lose their job, was perfect for the role and fulfilled it to perfection. They are one of the key reasons that the SSC was implemented effectively and operated well once in place.

Managing a finance department is no different than any other functional area. Each person has career objectives, and brings a set of skills and certain attitudes to their job. As the leader of the department, it is your job to match each person with their makeup, to meet your department objectives. The reality is that you don't want a department of superstars, because you will not be able to keep them all happy. I have always had the strategy to encourage the finance department to complete the month end (i.e. the routine part of the finance role) as quickly as possible. This was done for two reasons:

- Information, as it gets older, gets less relevant; accordingly, it is very important to get the info to the decision makers as soon as possible.
- The less time spent on the routine transaction processing, provides for more time on the strategic and support side of the finance function, where there could be more impact to the business.

This is just an example of strategizing your department, what you want to accomplish, and how you will manage your staff to do it. As a modern manager of people, I have found that first and foremost, most people are more effective if you level with them. They don't want platitudes. They want the truth. They want to know what is going on and why. If you explain decisions made by senior management, as well as the thought process and the final decision, they will be more than likely to accept it and implement it as best as they can, even if they disagree. They will have felt respected and, most importantly, shown how management has confidence in them by confiding in them. When possible, I would seek out their opinion before decisions had been made, which was even more effective. Any hardworking, intelligent, caring employee, more than anything, wants to be heard. Once you give them this respect, they will abide by almost any decisions.

The Positions in a Finance Department

Regardless of the size of the company, these are the typical positions in any finance department:

- Chief financial officer (CFO)/controller/director of finance (most senior position)
- Senior accountant
- Junior accountant
- Staff positions
- Analysts
- External vs internal accountants

Any finance department has any combination of these positions, with the number of each determined by the size of the business, the number of transactions done, and their complexity.

Chief financial officer, controller, director of finance. Any one of these positions is typically the most senior person in the finance department. The actual title given very much depends on the size of the company, whether it is a subsidiary as part of a multinational, and the actual experience of the individual in the position. Regardless of the title, the rule is that the most qualified financial professional in the company holds this position. This will mean they likely are a designated accountant, they have many years of experience in such a position, and are part of the management team. It will be their responsibility to be the custodian of all the financial records for the company, and provide the financial expertise to the management team and/or owner.

Senior accountant or junior accountant. People in these roles are usually but not always designated accountants. This means that they have done a sufficient amount of schooling to know about accounting, and they have also passed whatever the appropriate exams are in the jurisdiction to be able to have the accountant designation letters after the name. People in these positions are usually the ones who review any of the unusual transactions, and ensure that the accounting treatment for said transaction is done appropriately. They are also usually the people who will supervise the staff positions, because they themselves, in the recent past, have been doing the staff role, and have now been elevated to an accountant role.

Staff positions. These are positions that are usually held by people who are more clerical in nature; they may have been bookkeepers but are not designated accountants. They will handle the transaction processing for companies in either the accounts payable and/or accounts receivable area. They may or may not be young and just starting out with the aspirations to becoming accountants, or they could be somebody with many years' experience, who has no ambition to become an accountant and is happy just handling transaction processing.

Analyst. These are positions held by people that are usually very educated and do not wish, nor aspire, to be accountants. In many cases they have an MBA and thus have excellent analytical minds and sophisticated knowledge to use financial software to do analysis.

External accountant vs internal accountant. The positions, so far, are all *internal* financial staff. There is a distinction between internal financial staff and external accountants. Internal financial staff are as named above. External accountants are typically part of a CPA firm that offers accounting services and advice. CPA firms will have a range of accountants, from newly graduated financial students, up to very experienced CPAs. A CPA firm is basically an accounting service company that provides accounting, taxation, and other related financial services to companies. Most companies recognize that it is much more economical to have their own finance staff, and then they augment this with the external accountants. Depending on whether the company is public or private, it will have a large impact on the role of the external accountants. When a company is public, it must have an audit, which the external accounting firm performs as its primary duty. It may then provide other financial services at the discretion of management. When a company is private, it does not require an audit; and in fact, if it is confident with its internal finance staff, it may not use an external accounting firm. This, though, is rare. Usually, companies will have an external accounting firm to assist their CFO as required. Typically, this is on difficult accounting issues and income tax matters (more about income tax in Chapter 11).

Role of the External Accountant

If you are a public company, you are required to have an audit performed by accredited accountants, who make an opinion on your financial statements that are reported to your shareholders and the securities commission with which your company is registered. Only a professional accountant who is licensed to perform an audit can do so and render an opinion for public companies. The external accountant who is licensed to perform an audit is referred to as an auditor.

If you are a private company, then you do not sell shares to the public. You are not listed on a stock exchange and, thus, there is not a requirement from the shareholders' perspective to have an audit. Your banker or any debt holder may require an audit, and this will be specified in your loan documents. In the event of an audit for a private company, it is no different than the audit for a public company, except there may be some additional reporting specified in the loan documents that the auditor would attest to.

I have used the word, *attest.* In the audit context, this means that the auditor confirms that the financial statements as presented are true. However, truth is not absolute. When an auditor confirms that the financial statements are accurate, this means within a level of materiality. In other words, accuracy is not to the penny or dollar, or even thousand dollars. It is the amount in a certain magnitude, that if you knew this amount, it would change your decision. So, materiality, as an amount, is different for each company, regardless of size.

When an auditor performs an audit, he/she reviews the financial statements in terms of the numbers and the notes. In order to do this, he/she looks at all your accounting records. He/she will select some of the transactions as recorded in your accounting records to actually see the original documents (i.e. vendor invoices, sales invoices, shipping documents, purchase orders, contracts, correspondence, and any other documentation that he/she deems necessary to ensure the data in the financial statements is correct subject to materiality). He/she will talk to employees and ask questions to validate that the data corresponds to what he/she is told. He/she will communicate in writing with external parties, like suppliers, and contractual parties, to confirm information. The auditor has methods to perform the audit, developed through his/her unique skills as an auditor of many other clients, and as required in the auditing standards of his/her profession. In addition to the review of the financial transactions, the auditor maintains his/her knowledge on the latest accounting standards on presenting information. This ensures that not only are the financial statements presenting the financial info fairly according to the factual transactions, but they are presented according to the latest accounting standards.

Typically, every company has its own finance department with varying levels of accounting staff who are responsible for the preparation of the financial information of the company. Most accredited accountants were auditors early in their career, and then they decided to work inside a company instead of being an external party as an auditor. The internal accountant becomes very knowledgeable about the company's ongoing operations, and provides financial advice on a regular basis. Since this becomes the focus, usually their knowledge about accounting standards becomes less relevant, and they start relying more on the external accountant to provide this knowledge. Accordingly, the internal accountant likely still realizes when there is an accounting issue but is not totally up to date on the latest accounting standards, and this is why the external accountant, who deals with these matters on a regular basis, is called upon.

If you have accredited accountants within your finance department, they are no less qualified than the external accountant. The work that they do is different; it is more related to the ongoing business needs, and less about the annual financial statements.

As a business owner, you should give your internal accountant freedom to consult with the external accountants on an ongoing basis throughout the year. This ensures that any issues are dealt with appropriately at the time of the transaction and do not wait for the year-end audit. It also allows the internal and external accountants to work together rather than potentially being adversaries at the year end.

Managing the Finance Department

The most important message I can provide in managing a finance department is to listen to them. Help them with their career. Be a mentor, not just a boss. I found that by having a regular review with them once a month, with no time limit, where we talked about their work and also their progress in their career or areas of work development, I maximized their potential.

Of course, to be operating at this level requires a strong work performance process that not only provides the feedback on their past work performance, but sets a path of what they will do in the next year. I am sure, if you have been a manager of people, you will have learned that most people will hold themselves up to a standard higher than any boss will. Accordingly, I always had each person write their own work performance review, and then I modified it, usually with a better rating and a few less challenges in the future, since I wanted them to succeed. Nothing breeds success like more success. Setting a difficult challenge is all in keeping to the norm of building capabilities, but if it is too difficult and likely unachievable, you probably create a feeling of failure. So I believe that it is better to slightly reduce a target and have it met, rather than set an almost impossible target, come close, but not achieve it. All these thoughts are not unique to a finance department. These are just good HR principles. However, because most people in finance have already studied to be a professional accountant, they are achievers and looking for more. They don't usually rest on their laurels. As the leader, you need to find what excites them in finance, what they are good at, and then provide that opportunity for them to experience this. I have never seen a finance department where all the work is done, including my own. So it is usually pretty easy to find some new work for an aspiring finance professional, even if you may have to go to your boss and ask for a special project. Isn't that a great opportunity, to go to your boss and say, "Person X wants to do Y. Will you allow them to do this work to get this experience?" Would you see very many senior managers refusing this offer?

I have been lucky enough to work with many exemplary finance professionals, who I mentored, during my career. Many of them have now gone on to great successes in their career. In hindsight, they all tell me the same message: "Thank you for pushing me to realize my potential." I do believe finance professionals are uniquely qualified to develop because of their training and the typical stereotype of being thorough, disciplined, and ethical; and thus, whether you are their leader or you have a finance department in your company, my final piece of advice is, "Don't look at your finance staff as bean counters; they can do so much more, if you give them the opportunity to do so, and you encourage them."

The next chapter discusses speciality topics like value-adding activities and forensic accounting.

Chapter Highlights

- I have always found that to have a finance department that is more than just a bunch of accountants, it requires firstly to get the routine part of the job (transaction processing, preparing standard financial information) done as quickly as possible. This then maximizes the time available to do value-adding activities.
- Every finance department has some or all of these positions, depending on the size of the company and the complexity of the business: chief financial officer, senior accountant, junior accountant, bookkeeper, clerical positions, and analysts. The background and qualifications of each position are discussed.
- Your external accountants' main role is usually an audit if you are a public company, or if you are a private company with debt covenants that require an audit. The role of the external accountants is to attest to the accuracy of the financial statements subject to materiality.
- My most effective means to manage finance departments has been to act more as a mentor than a boss, by helping them with their career. This meant giving them work assignments that best used their skills or gave them opportunities to learn new skills.

Chapter 10 – Special Projects

Analysis, Forensic Accounting

- Value-adding activities
- What is analysis?
- Forensic accounting

Value-Adding Activities

A top-performing finance department does much more than keep the books. I trust that as you read this chapter, you have appreciated all the different aspects in the previous chapters, about different things that your finance department is doing. In order to perform additional duties, a well-run finance department must close the books on a regular monthly schedule, in a timely manner, so that there is additional time available in the remainder of the month to do special projects.

Special projects can take many forms. Some of the typical examples are:

- Analysis of historical financial information
- Using historical information to project future trends
- Analyzing spending that is contrary to budgeted performance
- Evaluating potential new projects for the business
- Managing compliance activities before there is a potential issue
- Special assignments from senior management
- System changes/improvements

Any of these activities are likely to yield business improvements. That is why top-performing finance departments complete the month-end routine as soon as possible, so they can maximize the amount of time spent on these potential opportunities. In fact, it is an even better idea to establish special projects at the beginning of the year, which are spread out over the calendar year, so that the finance team can better plan its own work assignments to maximize these opportunities.

What is Analysis?

In Chapter 5, there was discussion about the typical financial analysis. That discussion oriented around the types of analysis that accountants typically do from the financial records. Talking about analysis in this chapter is about much more sophisticated business analysis.

Even though we now have the advent of many sophisticated software programs that can provide high level analysis, most companies do not in fact take much advantage of this. I think that senior executives don't realize the abilities, both through the skill set of the individuals in their finance department and/or tools in the matter of software that would permit finance professionals to do an extensive amount of analysis, which would be useful to the business. The limiting factor is not the people in finance, nor the software; senior executives are not doing enough "what if" thinking. The true entrepreneur is always dreaming up new things; and typically, through their powerful leadership, just decides to go ahead. A large part of this, in the past, was because they had no data, and they just had to take the risk and make a decision. Today, there's no lack of data; ask for it. This is where you can make better use of your finance department. Share with them your dream/aspirational ideas, and let them be the ones to work through the possible analysis of the end result of these activities. This would then provide a basis of some factual information rather than decisions made on instincts.

Forensic Accounting

The dictionary definition is: *"the use of accounting skills to investigate fraud or embezzlement, and to analyze financial information for use in legal proceedings."*

There's both good news and bad news about forensic accounting. The good news is that the sophistication of analytic tools and accounting software permits the finance professional to investigate and evaluate large amounts of data in a very quick period of time. The bad news is that the same tools and accounting software permits those who wish to perpetrate fraud to be more sophisticated in being able to do so. The point is, we have better mouse traps, but we also have smarter mice.

Accordingly, the activity of forensic accounting has now become a specialty in and of itself. There are professional accountants who have experience working in the forensic sphere and have decided to now only work in this area, and thus have become specialists in it. This is good news for the good guys. This means that if you have any suspicions about potential fraud being committed in your company, there are professionals you can hire who are experts at potentially ferreting out the circumstances quickly. Unfortunately, one class of people, who are the major culprits at perpetrating fraud, are other financial professionals—typically your senior trusted professional in your company. This is probably another reason why the specialty of forensic accounting has arisen, because the detectives of fraud need to be in fact better than the perpetrators—and the perpetrators are pretty skilled. Sadly to say, if the C-suite executive has suspicions, they really need to go to an external party to determine whether there is fraud, because in fact it could be, and many of the times is, an internal member of the finance team.

There are some fundamentals that a C-suite executive/owner should employ to better protect their company from fraudulent activity, particularly by their internal finance professionals:

• Financial statements should be prepared on a timely basis.
• Bank reconciliations should be done monthly and be part of the normal monthly financial routine.
• Bank reconciliations should be signed off by a C-suite executive.
• Cheques over a material amount should always be signed by the C-suite executive.
• Any material variances to the budget, on a line-by-line basis, should be thoroughly explained.

There should be a monthly meeting between the C-suite executive/owner and the CFO, who would present the monthly financial statements and be available for any and all questioning.

The final chapter provides useful tax advice. No financial book would be complete without tax information, and this book is no exception.

Chapter Highlights

- The best run finance departments do the routine tasks quickly, so that the maximum amount of time and effort is devoted to value-adding activities. I suggest that your finance department should have MBOs at the beginning of the year, outlining projects to be done that will yield business improvement. This is the best way for a finance department to be more than bean counters.

- Use your finance team to perform "what if" analysis. This is a powerful tool that is made possible with many software programs, and the improved skill of finance professionals to use this software.

- Forensic accounting has become a major new discipline area in finance because of the sophistication of fraud. We need people skilled in having the tools and experience to find the fraud. Don't be shy about hiring a forensic expert if you have any suspicions about anyone in your company.

Chapter 11 – Specialty Areas

Income Taxes, Insurance

- Ongoing decision making
- Compliance
- External accountants/experts
- Insurance

Ongoing Decision Making

Income taxes are a favorite topic at cocktail hours. Everybody has some story with which they wish to impress their friends/colleagues. The sad part is that many people listening to such stories potentially walk away, and if it was a piece of advice that does supposedly save taxes, they then implement it in their own company. Income tax advice is one of those areas where the value of the advice is worth what you pay for it. In other words, if you got something for free, that's what it is worth—nothing.

The fundamental rule of income tax is, "Every person has the right to arrange their affairs in such a manner as to avoid taxes but not to *evade* taxes."

Unfortunately, many business people don't know this rule, or take such unwise positions as to bend over backwards to do everything about avoiding and then potentially evading taxes. The reality is, if you're paying taxes, it means you're making money. If you operate from a position of gratitude, then you should be thankful you're making money, and not begrudge the fact that you are paying taxes into your democratically elected government, who then decides the most appropriate way to use this revenue for the good of our society. I know this is a business book, but I felt compelled to provide some socialistic comments.

The real point here is that many business people get hung up about income taxes in their decision making. I have read many times, and been the recipient of some wise mentors who gave me this simple fundamental advice: *"Do whatever analysis, investigation, and due diligence that you deem appropriate when making a decision, and based on those findings, make your decision. Do not let income tax determine your business decision."* Once you've made your decision, then by all means follow the fundamental rule of income tax, which is to arrange your affairs in such a manner as to minimize the amount of income tax.

Compliance

When discussing the issue of compliance with the income tax rules, I have to caution you that you are entitled to arrange your affairs in such a way as to minimize taxes, but do not evade them. Provided you have consulted with experts who provide you with the best manner in which you can minimize the taxes, or in fact take a position that is defensible to minimize tax, then you can proceed. However, do not do a business transaction if you are knowingly not following the rules. This is a simple term, called *lack of compliance*. Even though our system in Canada is a self-assessment one for both personal and corporate levels, when you don't comply with the rules, it seems that, ultimately, this doesn't work at some point in the future. So, don't do it.

Typically, what happens is that there's more than one way in which a transaction can be organized. There is the preferred way to do it, from a CRA perspective, and a possible position that provides a better income tax result. This then brings us back to the fundamental rule of organizing your affairs in such a way as to minimize tax. This is totally legitimate, provided you have in fact consulted with experts who have given you such an opinion and the manner in which to organize your affairs. I see too many times where C-suite executives/owners either avoid getting advice or ignore it, to their peril. There is nothing wrong with taking a position that may not be the most appropriate accordingly to CRA, if there is a position that provides a better result, as long as the better tax result does have some defensible justification.

Assuming you do get the expert advice, and it is giving you the tax treatment that is more beneficial to you, follow it exactly as provided. In other words, whatever organizational structures/timing are advised, follow them fully. Do not cut corners.

External Accountants/Experts

In numerous sections in this book, I've talked about your external accountants and their role. Providing fundamentally wise income tax advice is typically one of the most used areas in which their advice is sought. This occurs for a number of reasons:

- They have tax advisors in the firm who do nothing but provide tax advice.
- They have many clients for whom they provide tax advice, who share many of the same issues that you are contemplating.

- They have a relationship with CRA, so that if they are providing advice to you, it is more likely that CRA will accept it in the event that any questions arise.
- They can use their relationship with CRA, in the event that there are formal questions posed, to act on your behalf.

Notwithstanding the earlier comment in this chapter, about making business decisions regardless of income tax considerations, it is wise in the decision making process to involve your external accountants and seek their guidance. Specifically, by providing them with the potential likely decision, they can advise you of any issues you should be aware of prior to making the decision, so that in your negotiations, these considerations can be dealt with at an earlier stage.

Aside from involving the external accountants in specific business decisions, the area where they can best provide their expertise is in the ongoing structures of your company, or of any trust or holding companies. On operating from the basis of arranging your affairs in the way best to minimize tax, the likely best path involves the legal structure of a transaction, the ownership structure, and the way in which the income earned by your company is paid to you, the owner.

Professional Advisors

Aside from your external accountants, there are other external advisors who should be considered part of your management team, even though they are not an employee.

Lawyer: It is always wise to have a lawyer, whether they are a sole practitioner or a firm with speciality areas, as your retained advisor. Don't wait until you are being sued, or need to sue some other party, to then look to hire a lawyer. Yes, they are not cheap, but I can assure you that the money spent on a lawyer will either be necessary to meet regulation issues, or will be money very well spent to maximize a payout or minimize your responsibility when you are in the wrong. They should be part of your advisor team, who knows and understands your business, so that when you call upon them, you do not need to spend a lot of time providing background info so that they can work effectively.

Insurance Broker: They are specialists in knowing all about the proper insurance coverage for your business. They have the relationship with all the major insurance companies, so they will get you the best coverage, at the lowest cost possible, based on market conditions. In order to get the right coverage at the best price, work with your insurance broker to raise all possible issues, so that either you don't need insurance or he/she goes out and gets the coverage. This is one of the most important manners in which you will not have the worst case scenario of making a claim and the insurance company denying the claim, because in your view, they found a loophole. The way to avoid loopholes is to discuss all possible risks with your insurance broker, and let them get the coverage that you need. A recent example will highlight this thinking. Cyber risk has been heightened in recent years, so there is now cyber insurance. My insurance broker raised the subject, and then we had an internal management discussion to review the potential risk. We then took out coverage that gave the owners peace of mind in case anything happened. This was done so that we didn't have some surprise about a cyber attack, and then have to ask, "Why are we not insured?"

Benefits Advisor: The size of your company will dictate whether this is handled internally by your HR staff or by an independent consultant who specializes in benefit plans. Similar to the insurance broker, benefit consultants have relationships with the insurers who provide benefit plans, and thus will get you the right plan for your company.

Other: There are many functional areas for which to hire advisors: marketing, logistics, customer service, HR, regulatory, and mergers and acquisitions. Suffice to say, you should get referrals for any business advisor you hire and add to your team, and put them through an interview process similar to that when you hire employees. It is common today that many experts in a functional area are now working as independent consultants, and you can hire them on an as-needed basis. This is very advantageous to get what you need, when you need it, without having to create a full-time employee position.

Board of Advisors: In private companies, there is no a board of directors; yet, particularly in owner/manager businesses, this is a wise addition to the management team. These are people who have a long career in their functional area, and have expertise and contacts that may not exist in your management team, which could be helpful to your business. Usually, they are on a monthly retainer, and thus you use them as much as you need, when you need them.

Insurance

Insurance is a wise investment to make, to protect your business from risks that, if they occurred, could put your business in severe difficulty. These are the typical areas of coverage:

Property: These are the physical assets, like buildings, furniture, and inventory. If they were damaged or stolen, or destroyed in a fire, they would have to be replaced at their cost value. Regardless of your own risk tolerance, if you have any bank debt, your banker will require this insurance as part of your loan arrangements.

Liability: In today's litigious environment in North America, you cannot take the risk of operating without liability insurance, because one legal suit, even if not warranted, could wipe out your business. Liability insurance covers you for being sued for activities that were generated by your products/services/employees in carrying your business, and the legal fees to defend your company. The legal fees alone, if you are not covered, aside from the distraction to management, would be a severe drain on any business. You will also find that many businesses that deal with you will require you to provide evidence of liability insurance as a condition of doing business with you.

Business Interruption: This is insurance to reimburse you for the costs and lost profits if your business is shut down for forces beyond your control (e.g., fire). This is relatively cheap insurance, and if you were in the unfortunate position to meet the criteria to have a claim, you would be exceedingly happy that you have coverage; otherwise, an insured event, if not covered, could bankrupt your business.

Cyber: This is a new insurance that has been provided to the market in the last few years, due to the detrimental impact of hackers and what they can do to your business. This is also a relatively cheap insurance, yet its coverage and expertise provided by the insurance company, if you were making a claim, is invaluable.

Chapter Highlights

- The fundamental rule about income tax is, "Every person has the right to arrange their affairs in such a manner as to avoid taxes, but not to evade tax." Don't let tax be the tail that wags the dog. Make your best business decision first, and then arrange that business decision with the best possible tax position.

- Use professional tax advisors whenever there is a large transaction that has many different tax treatments. Follow the advice as given; don't only partially follow it.

- Your external accountants are usually your best tax advisors because they have the right expertise, they know your business, you have a relationship with them, and they have creditability with CRA.

- There are many external advisors that you would be wise to employ on an as- needed basis, to maximize the best results for your company:

  • Lawyer
  • Insurance broker
  • Benefits advisor
  • Board of advisors
  • Functional area experts in HR, IT, logistics, and marketing

Glossary of Terms

Term	Description	Page
Accounts Payable	The amount you owe to your suppliers	8
Accounts Receivable	The amount that your customers owe you	8
Attest	A consulting service in which an external accountant expresses a conclusion about the reliability of information that is the responsibility of someone else	115
Balance Sheet	Statement of financial position for a company, of its assets, liabilities, and owner's equity	3
Budget	Future estimate of the company's financial statements that becomes the standard for the fiscal year when reviewing the actual results (usually just the income statement)	72
Cash Flow	Collections less disbursements	34
CRA	Canada Revenue Agency: the department within the Canadian government's finance department, which administrates the taxation system.	17
Financial Forecast	Same as a budget but done during the year as an update to the budget	72
Flash Sales	Sales for the prior month, reported on the first morning after the month is over. Described as *flash*, because this reporting is usually done before the finance department has completed their procedures, to ensure the sales are reconciled to all the records.	48
Forensic Accounting	The use of accounting skills to investigate fraud or embezzlement, and to analyze financial information for use in legal proceedings	124
Income Statement	Statement of revenue less expenses, for a period of time	49

KPI	Key performance indicator: the specific measures that senior management has decided are the most important to the success of the business, and these are usually reported on in a regular manner.	62
Metrics	A quantifiable measure that is used to track and assess the status of a specific business process.	62
Monthly Close	The schedule established by the finance department to close the books monthly.	46
Purchase Order (PO)	Document sent to a company that is a statement of the desire to buy, with the specifics of what is being bought, and for at what price. Signed by an authorized official of the buying company, POs are used as the simple medium of communication as a quasi-contract by the buying company.	32
Set of Books	The accounting records for a company	2
Sales Forecasting	This is the system to attempt to predict which products will be bought, in what quantities, by your customers.	87
SKU	Stock keeping unit. This is the term to describe an individual product in generic terms. Every product sold by a company is a SKU.	88
WPR	Work performance review. This is the process, usually annually, where a boss prepares an evaluation of an employee's performance.	100

Acknowledgements

Acknowledgements, in chronological order in my life:

Barry Razmov has been a lifetime good friend who has always been there for me, to keep me grounded in knowing my roots and the strong values we were taught as we grew up.

Pat Ryan, as the partner at my first accounting job, Thorne Riddell, who immediately welcomed me into the firm and was always one of my top supporters in the firm. He was particularly instrumental in me passing the uniform CA exam on my first attempt, because of his confidence in my abilities.

Jim Wood, as my first manager at Thorne Riddell, who took an immediate liking to me and was always there to smooth off some of my rough edges, as I was particularly politically incorrect early in my career. (Now I know when I am, whereas back then, I was just oblivious.) Jim became my true mentor throughout my career, to hone my technical accounting expertise, and has always been a true friend for life.

Dave Warner was another of my partners, at Thorne Riddell, who taught me the discipline and hard work needed to succeed in the CA business.

Arthur Rosenzweig, as a supervisor at Thorne Riddell, has always been a friend throughout life, to be more philosophical about life.

Mike Stayton, as my first boss outside of public accounting, and a key person to increase my awareness of being more than an accountant.

Robert Scolnick, as a boss who taught me how to use accounting in business.

Mike Levine started as a business colleague and has been a lifetime friend who has always brought humour to my life, while also being a wise business person who I could rely on at any time for sage advice.

Ron Moore, as my first boss at Spalding Canada, showed me how to be both a nice guy yet effective in business at the same time.

Tom Wright started as a business colleague and became my boss at Spalding Canada. He was the first boss to recognize my business acumen, and provided numerous opportunities to elevate myself into a senior business partner, and more than just the senior finance person in the company.

Acknowledgements

Mel Engle, as my first boss at Allergan, and the person who hired me at Allergan, was instrumental in acclimatizing me into a big corporation, and educating me on managing a corporate head office.

Sheldon Kovensky was my long-time boss at Allergan, and also recognized my business acumen and provided the opportunities to use and then actually put me in a non-finance operating role to show his confidence in me.

Mike Mooney, as my head office boss at Allergan, allowed me to be myself, and smoothed the way when I was outside the accepted political norm at Allergan.

Larry Gravel was one of my colleagues at Allergan, and we learned from each other as we are both out- of-the-box thinkers.

Marvin Haggith was truly my mentor for years. He was the recruiter who hired me at Allergan, and we became friends, and he was always the first person whose advice I sought outside of the company for business advice.

Brent Zylberberg cold-called me while at Allergan, to provide commercial real estate services, and after I hired him, we quickly became friends. Not only have we remained friends, I consider him to be one of my best life friends who is always there for me, in business and personal life situations, to keep me laughing and provide whatever support is needed at the time.

Toby Belman was the owner of The Canadian Institute, and as her CFO, it was my first CFO role in a private company. Toby provided me the full opportunity to operate in both a typical financial role and as a business advisor.

Marv Turk, as the president of Hy & Zel's, invited me in as his business partner, and always was interested in my advice. He listened to it and implemented it, which both gave me confidence in myself and the belief that we could save Hy & Zel's.

Polydor Strouthos, Cleon Strouthos, and Ray Dube, as the three partners at Labtician, have provided me with a wonderful work opportunity as I get to the latter stages of my work career, and have accepted many of my idiosyncrasies. Polydor, in fact, has shown his extreme loyalty, as early in his career, I was a finance mentor to him, and now he has blossomed into a truly wise president who is one of my great mentors and best friends.

Jack Corman is another business colleague, who is a good friend and provides wise business counsel, and he provided a professional work opportunity when he had his own company.

Arsalan Mohajer was a client to whom I provided financial consulting, and he was a very smart man who I am thankful provided many mentoring opportunities.

Jennifer Beale and Eileen Fauster, as good female friends who have been like the sisters I didn't have, who have given me personal support and advice on seeking a life partner .

Roman Turlo is a friend who has been a colleague in our continued quest for self-improvement, and has been a great source for personal support and advice on seeking a life partner.

Sunil Tulsiani is a mentor who has encouraged me to operate to my potential, and without this encouragement, I wouldn't have written this book.

Alan Noyek is a friend who has been a great source for personal support and advice on seeking a life partner.

Cora Cristobal, as a friend who has blazed the trail of an accountant, and who has become a leader in the business community—thus, providing me the example to follow—and who introduced me to Raymond Aaron, whose influence has been essential to write this book.

About the Author

Larry M. Cooper, CPA, is a well-seasoned finance executive with a panache of entrepreneurialism. He is the business partner that every CEO, owner/manager, and executive team requires to help grow their business and/or sustain their company in these difficult economic times.

Larry has a wealth of direct experience in many different industries (pharmaceutical, biologicals, CPG, food, retail, automotive), in all sectors of the economy (manufacturing, distribution, service, retail), operating in all of the different organization structures (public, private, owner managed, multinational), which he has acquired through his many years as a CFO.

Larry is an Author, having been one of the Experts who wrote in the International Best Seller *Achieve.*

Larry is available for either short-term assignments or ongoing consulting.

Contact Larry M. Cooper, CPA, who can help you grow your company profitably through his 5- step process:

Initial Consultation: review all aspects of your business
Identify: the areas for improvement
Investigate: these opportunities
Action Plan: implement the opportunities
Ongoing Business Meeting: to monitor implementing the opportunities

CONTACT LARRY SO YOU CAN BEGIN HIS
5-STEP PROCESS
Phone: 416-818-4217
Email: Larry@redtoblackcfo.com
Website: https://redtoblackcfo.com

Endorsements

Larry is a different CFO. He is creative and thinks out of the box, which sets him apart from most CFOs.

Larry has rewritten the acronym of CFO to mean Chief Fun Officer, because when your business is making lots of money, it's fun.

Larry has written the book *RedtoBlack*, which outlines all the typical fundamental areas and subjects handled in a finance department. This is especially important for non-financial executives who may not have the background in finance, and must rely extensively on their CFO. *RedtoBlack* will quickly accelerate your learning curve about what is important in a finance department, what questions to ask to get the most out of that department, and how to best deploy the finance team to add value to your business.

If you want YOUR business to spend less time in the Red and more time in the Black, then you must read this book. It will show you exactly how to organize your finance department. Get a copy for every member of your financial team, and tell them to follow Larry Cooper's brilliant advice. Once you and your team implement the *RedtoBlack* strategies, you'll be laughing all the way to the bank.

Robert G. Allen
Author of the New York Times bestsellers, *Creating Wealth,* *Nothing Down,* *Multiple Streams of Income* **and** *The One Minute Millionaire.*

Larry was my CFO when I first became a President. While my background was marketing and sales, I needed an experienced, skilled and trusted financial resource to bring balance and perspective to the Executive Team at Spalding. Larry delivered this in spades and was a key contributor to our success.

As a CFO he has a keen analytical mind and a practical style of management that he effectively uses to focus on business opportunities and/or problems first. Once the business issue is addressed, he then ensures that the accounting/financial requirements are properly managed and reported within the overall context of an organization's strategic plans and priorities.

Larry shares these special skills and more in this book. This know-how is fundamental to consistent and profitable business results. Anyone reading this, particularly Owners/Managers, will directly benefit from his first-hand work experience, his practical approach and his deep knowledge of business finance and accounting.

Tom Wright, Sports & Entertainment CSuite Executive.

I am a Business Owner for many years and yet I found information in Larry's book that I did not know and found interesting. I like that is in simple English.

Arthur Rosenzweig, Owner of St Clair Ice Cream

Larry has been the CFO in our business shortly after we bought it. He has been a trusted advisor in many facets of our business which has been an important contribution to our success.

As a CFO he is resourceful and knowledgeable in all operating financial matters that better support the business while maintaining proper financial integrity.

In this book the business owner reader gets the benefit of being introduced to the many processes and sound financial fundamentals that represent the disciplined approach for operating a business that Larry has implemented in our business and these that have been important to the good management of our business.

Polydor Strouthos, Owner of Labtician Ophthalmics Inc

Larry has created a book that would absolutely be of assistance to any Owner/Manager. I wish I had this book when I started my business many years ago. There are many things that Larry teaches in his book, that I would have done differently if I had the book, all for the better. It is a great reference source to any Owner/Manager.

Jack Cohen, Founder and Owner of IYB Consultants

Larry has written a well-organized and insightful book that is chock full of pragmatic, highly useful information gleaned from his years as a hands on accounting and senior finance executive. This book will be most helpful to new senior managers and business owners who need to understand the organization and essential functions of a finance department, without which they are unlikely to succeed. Experienced managers and business owners will also find Larry's book to be a useful quick reference and trouble-shooting manual to keep near at hand at all times.

Jack Corman, Founder and Past Owner of IRB Services